POPULATION EXCHANGE

POPULATION EXCHANGE

Jinnah Wanted Hijrat for all Muslims in India

PRAFULL GORADIA
& K R PHANDA

Vitasta

Published by
Vitasta Publishing Pvt Ltd
2/15, Ansari Road, Daryaganj
New Delhi-110 002
info@vitastapublishing.com

ISBN 978-93-86473-81-3

First Edition 2020
MRP ₹595

Cover and layout by Somesh Kumar Mishra
Printed by Vikas Computer and Printers, New Delhi

Contents

Why this Book?

IN 2003, I presented a volume called *Unfinished Agenda of the League* to Mr LK Advani at a special meeting held at the basement hall of the India International Centre Annexe. While acknowledging the book from the podium, he called it a new discovery. He did not hesitate to admit that he had, until then, not heard of an exchange of population. He was nearly 20 years old at Partition and was still at Karachi. Soon he became a *pracharak* of the Rashtriya Swayamsevak Sangh; yet, the subject was not discussed at the *bouddhiks* delivered at the *shakhas* he had attended. The late Devendra Swarup, a senior professor of history at Delhi University complimented me immediately and said that the book had been approved by the party boss. What more could a writer desire?

The book was self-published and did not get widely distributed, nor did it attract any debate or discussion. I have felt all these years that the subject needed to be put out again for more readers. The current century, as it began, seems progressively like the 20th century with similar minority demands despite the government at Delhi favouring, if not also pampering the Muslims. The Constitution of free India, released about two years after 15 August 1947, incorporates fundamental rights including Articles 25 to 30, which make the minorities almost superior to the majority and whose priorities are listed only as Directive Principles of Policy and not as fundamental rights. Yet Article 14 proclaims all citizens of India to be equal. Seven decades of Independent India are one crowded catalogue of contradictions and conflicts.

It is not widely known that Articles 25 to 30 owe their origin to communalism. The Constituent Assembly was elected in January 1946. On 13 December of the same year, Jawaharlal Nehru, as head of the interim government, moved, what was called, an Objective Resolution, whose aim was to appease the Muslim League in the hope that it would not press for partition. Remember, that no final decision had been taken on the grant of independence to India till 20 February 1947.

As it happened, the endeavour to appease the League failed, the country was divided and a Muslim homeland came into being. It is useful to recall that the Constituent Assembly had been elected on the basis of separate Muslim constituencies, then called separate electorates, and 85 per cent of the voters had voted for the League, whose single point manifesto then was Partition.

Cabinet Mission

Dr BR Ambedkar in his book *Thoughts on Pakistan* had written that between 1920 and 1940 there was a civil war between Hindus and Muslims. Fighting was mostly in the form of riots in many cities and towns of India. In March 1940, the Pakistan Resolution was passed at the Lahore session of the Muslim League. Inevitably, tempers did not cool thereafter. The 1940s was the most riot ridden decade which witnessed some of the most barbaric killings in human history.

As part of the run up to the partition of the country in 1947, on 9 February 1946, Sir Feroz Khan Noon, later to become a prime minister of Pakistan, happened to address the Muslim members of the Bihar legislative assembly at Patna. In the course of his speech, he said that if the Hindus came in the way of Muslims going to Pakistan, the latter would re-enact the violent orgies earlier perpetrated by Chengez Khan and Halaqu Khan. Mohammed Ali Jinnah was equally keen on the emigration of Muslims from Hindustan to the coming Pakistan, as were seven other top leaders of the Muslim League. Jinnah had written to Viceroy Lord Wavell pleading for an exchange of populations.

Dr Ambedkar had responded to the Pakistan Resolution in his book which was published early in 1941. He had endorsed Jinnah's proposal in principle with comprehensive arguments on a number of aspects of the country's vivisection. Other than him, Chakravarti Rajagopalachari was also in favour of a division. But by and large, the Hindus did not like the idea. In fact, they were as opposed to the idea as much as the Muslims were hell bent on it. Jinnah in his speech immediately preceding the Resolution had explained at length the reasons for wanting a separate homeland for Muslims.

Sardar Vallabhbhai Patel and Jawaharlal Nehru accepted the proposal although rather reluctantly, for two reasons. One was to avoid a civil war as was implicitly threatened by the Muslim Leaguers. Secondly, acceptance of Partition was one way of making the British depart from India soon, so that Indians would become free. But what prevented these two great leaders from lending an ear to the very clear views of Dr Rajendra Prasad who, incidentally, went on to become the President of India for two consecutive terms? This is particularly galling in the light of the Muslim League's demand for a homeland for Muslims in India, a Dar-ul-Islam and the proposal by MA Jinnah and his colleagues for a population exchange. Dr Prasad was consistent in his belief that those Muslims who (could not emigrate and) stayed back in Hindustan could do so as *aliens* with visas issued by New Delhi. It was obvious that Dr Prasad's views were ignored. On the other hand, Jinnah completely agreed with Dr Prasad. Had his views not been ignored, what an enormous difference it would have made to the peace and progress of Hindustan? The repeat in this century of what happened in the last one would not have taken place. In many ways, this is the crux of this volume. The rest is an elucidation of each development, each opinion, each readily available record and so on. All in all, it is the unfolding of a tragedy knowingly by the leaders of the time, especially Messrs. Mohandas Gandhi and Jawaharlal Nehru.

Mutual exchange of populations is not an unthinkable idea nor unworkable, though it may seem detestable to many. This is particularly so in the instance of partitions of countries in which two or more segments of the population reach the conclusion that they cannot coexist together and it is better for the interests and futures of both concerned to go their separate ways. The late M Mujeeb, who was later the Vice-Chancellor of the Jamia Millia Islamia University in Delhi, says in his memoirs that at a party given during the UN General Assembly session in 1949 he had the pleasure of being placed next to the Turkish representative. He looked at Mujeeb's name card, saw that he was a Muslim and at once asked, 'Are there still any Muslims in India?' The impression then created does not yet seem to have been removed and it is believed that the sub-continent had been divided between Muslims and Hindus, with all Muslims on the one side and all Hindus on the other. The Turkish representative no doubt had his own country's experience in mind, which entered into a mutually agreed exchange of population with Greece in 1922, which was carried out under international supervision. However, this was not implemented in India following Partition.

Mohammed Ali Jinnah believed that Hindus and Muslims

cannot co-exist in the same country. He explained at length in his speech, on 22 March 1940, supporting the Pakistan resolution at the Muslim League session the following day. This resolution spelt out the demands while the speech was their justification. Most Hindu leaders rejected Jinnah's view. To them 'undivided India' was dear. Conceptually, it is equally to us even today.

The reality on the ground over the decades since Independence has been nothing short of tragic. Regrettably, the tallest of leaders did not think twice before misleading other leaders and the people of India. For example, on the eve of his assassination, Gandhi categorically told Dr Syamaprasad Mookerji, in the presence of Dr Rajkumari Amrit Kaur that the partition had taken place not on the basis of religion but on the basis of territory. It was a territorial division; so asserted the Mahatma. On hearing about the Pakistan Resolution passed in the Lahore session of the Muslim League on 23 March 1940, Gandhi stated, 'Partition over my dead body'. In the course of a discussion the following year, in the same context, he said 'Everyone had a right to self-determination'. This meant that the Muslims had a right to secede from the rest of the country.

On release from prison in 1944, Gandhi approached Jinnah for a one-to-one conversation on the subject. The two leaders were both Kathiawadis, one from Porbandar and the other from Dhoraji, both knowing only two languages fluently, Gujarati and English, communicated flawlessly. They met frequently during September that year at Jinnah's imposing Marble

House at Malabar Hill, Bombay. Each meeting was recorded by both the leaders through exchange of letters. The essence of the outcome was that Jinnah insisted on the time sequence of Partition first and independence later. On the other hand, Gandhi wanted independence first and thereafter the division of the country as brothers shared inherited property.

Partition did take place when the Pakistan flag replaced the Union Jack at Karachi on 14 August 1947. Hindustan or the rest of India had to wait till the early hours of the next day. Divided India awoke to freedom a day later, presumably to satisfy Jinnah, it was that Partition took place first and Independence thereafter. However, between 15 August and 30 January, Gandhi did undertake a fast unto death in order to force the Nehru government remit Rs 550 million to Pakistan as part of its cash dues upon the country's vivisection. Nehru was reluctant, as a war was raging between the countries in the Kashmir Valley. Such was the vicarious commitment of the Mahatma to his Muslim brothers across the border. Pakistan today is an Islamic State. There is no minority problem in West Pakistan, now Pakistan while East Pakistan, now Bangladesh is being steadily drained of its Hindus. India on the other hand still has a population of about forty million then then and now 172 million. Muslims, besides other minorities, to protect and care for. Gandhiji particularly emphasized that the minorities were a sacred trust in the hands of the majority. It was a cause most dear to his heart. He lived for it-indeed he eventually died for it, says VP Menon.

The day before the Pakistan Resolution was passed at Lahore in 1940, Jinnah had given a long and detailed speech to justify how different Hindus were from Muslims, and therefore how indispensable a vivisection was for them to live in peace. An integral part of this essential separation was the conviction of Jinnah and his seven senior colleagues that an exchange of population was imperative, whereby all non-Muslims should vacate Pakistan and all Muslims across the border should immigrate to the new Muslim homeland, described by some Aligarh Muslim University luminaries as the 'new Medina'.

In his memorable book *A Stern Reckoning*, Justice GD Khosla, ICS, has lucidly argued why a population exchange was an integral part of Partition. If Muslims could live happily with Hindus in the same country, where was the need for a division?

We may briefly come back to Dr Ambedkar's *Thoughts on Pakistan*, wherein he sets out at length for what all reasons a partition was necessary, also outlining the two decades of civil war between Hindus and Muslims from 1920 to 1940. As a summing up, he wrote that an enemy is safer outside the country than within its borders.

Apparently, Nehru and his government could not see the connection between Jinnah's proposal of an exchange of population and the attacks on Hindus and Sikhs that began in Rawalpindi and spread to other parts of West Punjab in 1947. Alternatively, it chose to ignore the connection for his own political convenience. Nevertheless, what happened in West

Punjab was not a riot nor a mere pogrom, but a holocaust of Hindus and Sikhs, also causing a flood of refugees crossing the border into India. In comparison, the exodus of Muslims out of India was nominal, except perhaps from East Punjab. A not dissimilar tragedy unfolded in the eastern wing of Pakistan. The reverse flow out of West Bengal was negligible.

Ironically, Jinnah's proposal of an exchange of population, which fell on the deaf ears of Indian leaders, fructified in the form of an exodus from the new Medina. Even more ironical – and obnoxious was India's High Commissioner Sriprakasa being busy in persuading the just arrived Mohajirs from Banaras and other parts of UP to go back. His appeal to them was: "If you do not go back, who will operate the sari looms of Banaras?"

When the Hindu Dalits from Bihar and UP, who were working in Karachi, had to stay back against their own will, Sriprakasa was told by Pakistan's Prime Minister Liaqat Ali Khan to mind his own business. "If the Dalits leave, who will clean the streets of Karachi?" the Pak PM had asked.

In this context, Dr Rafiq Zakaria has quoted the interaction between MA Jinnah and the Cabinet Mission which visited India in 1946. Lord Pethick-Lawrence has said the following:

Mission asked Jinnah: "Do you realise that the Pakistan you are demanding will leave substantial Hindus under Muslim domination?"

Jinnah replied: "That will be so; but I will leave many more Muslims under Hindu domination in Hindustan."

Surprised at this reply the Mission said: "How does it then resolve Hindu-Muslim discord? It will only perpetuate the hostilities."

Jinnah persisted: "I will free at least two-third Muslims from Hindu domination."

The Mission told him: "And you will put more than that number of Hindus under Muslim domination. That is no solution."

Jinnah was adamant. He asserted: "That is the only solution if you don't want civil war."

The Mission was nonplussed at his stand and asked: "But should you adopt such a callous attitude towards the minorities in the two states, they will be in worse condition than the Muslims in united India – also the Muslims in divided India will be the worst sufferers."

Jinnah replied: "Their best protection will be the establishment of two strong states, neither of which will dare misbehave towards each other's minorities."

The Mission enquired: "You mean to say that the minorities will be hostages."

Jinnah said: "Exactly. If one state mistreats its minorities, the other state will retaliate against its minorities. It will be tit for tat."

Jinnah's Presidential Address*

WE ARE meeting today in our session after fifteen months. The last session of the All-India Muslim League took place at Patna in December 1938. Since then many developments have taken place. I shall first tell you briefly what the All-India Muslim League has had to face since the Patna session of 1938. You remember that one of the tasks, which were imposed on us and which are far from completed yet, was to organise Muslim Leagues all over India. We have made enormous progress during the last fifteen months in this direction. I am glad to inform you that we have established provincial Leagues in every province.

---

* Jamil-ud-din Ahmad, *Some Recent Speeches and Writings of Mr Jinnah*, vol. I, pp. 159-81.

The next point is that in every by-election to the Legislative Assemblies we had to fight powerful opponents. I congratulate the Muslims for having shown enormous grit and spirit throughout their trials. There was not a single by-election in which our opponents won against Muslim League candidates. In the last election to the UP Council, that is the Upper Chamber, the Muslim League's success was cent per cent. I do not want to weary you with details of what we have been able to do in the way of forging ahead in the direction of organizing the Muslim League. But I may tell you that it is going up by leaps and bounds.

Next, you might remember that we appointed a central committee of ladies at the Patna session. It is of very great importance to us, because I believe that it is absolutely essential for us to give every opportunity to our women to participate in this, our struggle of life and death. Women can do a great deal within their homes, even in purdah. We appointed this committee with a view to enabling them to participate in the work of the League. The objectives of this committee were: (1) to organise provincial and district Muslim Leagues; (2) to enlist a larger number of women to the membership of the Muslim League; (3) to carry on intensive propaganda amongst Muslim women throughout India in order to create in them a sense of greater political consciousness – because if political consciousness is awakened amongst our women, remember, our children will not have much to worry about; (4) to advise and guide them in all such matters as mainly rest on them for the uplift of Muslim society. This central committee, I am glad to say, started seriously and earnestly. It has done a great deal of useful work. I have no doubt that when we come to deal with its report of work done we shall really feel grateful to it for all the services that it has rendered to the Muslim League.

From January 1939, right up to the declaration of the war, we had to face many difficulties. We had to face the Vidya Mandir in Nagpur. We had to face the Wardha Scheme all over India. We had to face ill-treatment and oppression of Muslims in the Congress-governed provinces, and in some of the Indian States such as Jaipur and Bhavnagar. We had to face a vital issue that arose in the small State of Rajkot. Rajkot was made the acid test of its strength by the Congress and this would have affected one-third of India. Thus the Muslim League had to face all along various issues from January 1939 up to the time of the declaration of the war. Before the war was declared, the greatest danger to the Muslims of India was the possible inauguration of the federal scheme for the Central Government.

We knew what machinations were going on, but the Muslim League was stoutly resisting them in every direction. We felt that we could never accept the dangerous scheme for a Federal Central Government embodied in the Government of India Act, 1935. I am sure that we have made no small contribution towards persuading the British Government to abandon that scheme of Federal Government. You know that the British are a very obdurate people. They are also very conservative and although they are very clever, they are slow in understanding.

After the war was declared, the Viceroy naturally wanted help from the Muslim League. It was only then that he realised that the Muslim League was a power, for it will be remembered that up to the time of the declaration of the war, the Viceroy never thought of me but of Gandhi and Gandhi alone. I have been the leader of an important party in the Central Legislature for a considerable time, larger than the one I have the honour to lead at present, the Muslim League Party.

Yet the Viceroy never thought of me before. Therefore, when I got this invitation from the Viceroy, along with Mr Gandhi, I wondered within myself why I had so suddenly been promoted. Then I concluded that the answer was the 'All-India Muslim League' whose President I happen to be. I believe that was the worst shock that the Congress High Command has ever received, because it challenged their sole authority to speak on behalf of India. And it is quite clear from the attitude of Mr Gandhi and his High Command that they have not yet recovered from that shock.

My point is that I want you to realise the value, the importance, and the significance of organising yourselves. I will not say anything more on the subject.

A great deal yet remains to be done. I am sure from what I can see and hear that Muslim India is now conscious and awake, and the Muslim League has grown into such a strong institution that it cannot be destroyed by anybody, whoever he might be. Men may come and men may go, but the League will live forever.

Now, coming to the period after the declaration of the war, our position was that we were between the devil and the deep sea. But I do not think that the devil or the deep sea is going to get away with it. We stand unequivocally for the freedom of India. But it must be freedom for all India and not freedom for one section or, worse still, for the Congress caucus and slavery for the Muslims and other minorities.

Situated as we are in India, we naturally have learnt from our past experience. Particularly from the experiences of the last two and a half years in the Congress-governed provinces, we have learnt many lessons. We are, therefore, now, very apprehensive and can trust nobody. I think it is a wise rule for everyone not to trust anybody too much. Sometimes we are led to trust people but when we find in actual experience that our trust has been betrayed, surely that ought to be sufficient lesson for any man not to continue to trust those who have betrayed him.

Ladies and gentlemen, we never thought that the Congress High Command would act in the manner in which they actually did in the Congress-governed provinces. I never dreamt that they would ever come down so low as that. I never could believe that there would be a "gentlemen's agreement" between the Congress and the Britishers. Although we cried hoarse, week in and week out, the British Governors were supine and the Governor-General was helpless. We reminded them of their special responsibilities to us and to the other minorities and the solemn pledges they had given to us. But all that was a dead letter. Fortunately, Providence came to our help and that "gentlemen's agreement" was broken and the Congress, thank Heavens, went out of office. I think they are regretting their resignations very much. The bluff has been called. So far, so good. I appeal to you, with all the earnestness that I can command, to organise yourselves in such a way that you should depend upon none, only on your own inherent strength. That is your best safeguard, your only safeguard. Depend upon yourselves. That does not mean that you should have ill-will or malice towards others. In order to safeguard your rights and interests you must create strength in yourselves so that you may be able to defend yourselves. That is all that I wish to urge.

Now, what is our position with regard to the future Constitution? It is that as soon as circumstances permit or immediately after the war at the latest, the whole problem of India's Constitution must be examined *de novo* and the Act of 1935 must go once and for all. We do not believe in asking the British Government to make declarations. These declarations are really of no use. You cannot possibly succeed in getting the British Government out of this land by asking them to make declarations. However, the Congress asked the Viceroy to make a declaration. The Viceroy said, "I have made the declaration." The Congress said, "No, no; we want another kind of declaration. You must declare and at once, that India is free and independent with the right to frame its own Constitution through a Constituent Assembly to be elected on the basis of adult franchise or as Iowa franchise as possible.

This Assembly will, of course, satisfy the minorities' legitimate interests." MrGandhi says that if the minorities are not satisfied, then he would be willing that some tribunal of the highest and most impartial character should decide the dispute.

Now, apart from the impracticable nature of this proposal – being historically and constitutionally absurd toask the ruling power to abdicate in favour of a Constituent Assembly, suppose we do not agree to the franchise according to which the Assembly is to be elected, or suppose we, the solid body of Muslim representatives, do not agree with the non-Muslim majority in the Assembly, what will happen? It is said that we have no right to disagree with anything that this Assembly may do in framing a national Constitution for this huge subcontinent, except in those matters which may be germane to safeguards for the minorities. So, we are given the privilege to disagree only with regard to, what may strictly be called, safeguards of the rights and interests of minorities. We are also given the privilege to choose our own representatives by separate electorates.

Now this proposal is based on the assumption that as soon as this Constitution comes into operation the British hand will disappear. Otherwise there will be no meaning in it. Of course, Mr Gandhi says that the Constitution will decide whether the British will disappear and, if so, to what extent. In other words, his proposal comes to this: first, give me the declaration that we are a free and independent nation, then I will decide what

I should give you back! Does Mr Gandhi really want complete independence for India when he talks like this? But whether the British disappear or not, it follows that extensive powers must be transferred to the people. In the event of there being a disagreement in the Constituent Assembly between the majority and the Muslims, in the first instance, the question is, who will appoint the tribunal? And suppose an agreed tribunal is possible and it gives a decision, who will, may I ask, be there to see that it is implemented and carried out in accordance with the terms of the award? And who will see that it is honoured in practice, for, we are told, the British will have parted with their power, completely or mainly? What then will be the sanction for the enforcement of the award? We come back to the same answer: the Hindu majority will do it – and will it be with the help of British bayonets or Mr Gandhi's Ahimsa? Can we trust either anymore? Besides, ladies and gentlemen, can you imagine that a question of this character involving a contract, upon which the future Constitution of India would be based and affecting 90 million Muslims, can be decided by means of a judicial tribunal? Still that is the proposal of the Congress.

Before I deal with what Mr Gandhi said a few days ago, I shall refer to the pronouncements of some of the other Congress leaders, each one speaking with a different voice. Mr Rajagopalachariar, the ex-Prime Minister of Madras, says that the only panacea for Hindu-Muslim unity is joint electorates. This is his prescription as one of the great doctors of the Congress organisation! Babu Rajendra Prasad, on the other hand, only a few days ago said, "Oh, what more do the Muslims want?" I will read out to you his words. Referring to the minority question he says: "If Britain would concede our right of self-determination, surely all these differences would disappear." How will our differences disappear? He does not enlighten us about it. But he continues: "But so long as Britain remained and held power, the differences would continue to exist. The Congress has made it clear that the future Constitution will be framed not by the Congress alone but by the representatives of all political parties and religious groups. The Congress has gone further and declared that the minorities can have their representatives elected for this purpose by separate electorates, though the Congress regards separate electorates as an evil. It will be representatives of all the peoples of this country, irrespective of their religions and political affiliations, who will be deciding the future Constitution of India and not this or that party. What better guarantee can the minorities have?" So, according to Babu Rajendra Prasad, the moment we enter the Assembly, we shall shed all our political affiliations, and religions and everything else. This is what Babu Rajendra Prasad said as late as 18th March, 1940.

This is what Mr Gandhi said on 20th March, 1940: "To me Hindus, Muslims, Parsis, Harijans are all alike, I cannot be frivolous" – but I think he is frivolous – "I cannot be frivolous when I talk of Quaid-i-Azam Jinnah. He is my brother." The only difference is this, that brother Gandhi has three votes and I have only one vote! "I would be happy indeed if he could keep me in his pocket." I do not know really what to say to this latest offer of his. "There was a time when I could say that there was no Muslim whose confidence I did not enjoy. It is my misfortune that it is not so today." Why has he lost the confidence of the Muslims today, may I ask, ladies and gentlemen?

"I do not read all that appears in the Urdu press, but perhaps I get a lot of abuse there. I am not sorry for it. I still believe that without a Hindu-Muslim settlement there can be no *Swaraj*," Mr Gandhi has been saying this now for the last 20 years. "You will perhaps ask in that case why do I talk of a fight. I do so because it is to be a fight for a Constituent Assembly."

He is fighting the British. But may I point out to Mr Gandhi and the Congress that they are fighting for a Constituent Assembly which the Muslims cannot accept, in which the Muslims will be one against three. In that way, by the counting of heads, the Muslims say that they will never be able to come to an agreement with the Hindus, which will be a real agreement from the heart, which will enable them to work as friends. Therefore, this idea of a Constituent Assembly is objectionable. Mr Gandhi says that he is fighting for a Constituent Assembly, and not fighting the Muslims at all. He says, "I do so because it is to be a fight for a Constituent Assembly. If Muslims who come to the Constituent Assembly" – mark the words, "who come to the Constituent Assembly through Muslim votes" he is first forcing us to come to that Assembly and then says, "declare that there is nothing common between Hindus and Muslims then alone would I give up all hope, but even then I would agree with them because they read the Koran and I have also studied something of that Holy Book."

So he wants the Constituent Assembly for the purpose of ascertaining the views of the Muslims and if they do not agree with him then he will give up all hope, but even then he will agree with us! Well, I ask you, ladies and gentlemen, is this the way to show real, genuine desire, if there exists any, to come to a settlement with the Muslims? Why does not Mr Gandhi, as I have suggested to him more than once, and I repeat it again from this platform, why does not Mr Gandhi honestly acknowledge now that the Congress is a Hindu Congress, that he does not represent anybody except the solid body of Hindu people? Why should not Mr Gandhi be proud to say, "I am a Hindu, the Congress has solid Hindu backing."

I am not ashamed of saying that I am a Muslim. I am right and I hope and believe, even a blind man must have been convinced by now, that the Muslim League has the solid backing of the Muslims of India. Why then all this camouflage? Why all these machinations? Why all these methods to coerce the British to overthrow the Muslims? Why this declaration of noncooperation? Why this threat of civil disobedience? And why fight for a Constituent Assembly for the sake of ascertaining whether the Muslims agree or do not? Why not come as a Hindu leader, proudly representing your people, and let me meet you proudly representing the Muslims? This is all that I have to say so far as the Congress is concerned.

So far as the British Government is concerned, our negotiations with it are, as you know, not yet concluded. We had asked for assurances on several points. We have made some advance, at any rate, with regard to one point, which is this. You remember our demand was that the entire problem of the future Constitution of India should be examined *de novo*, and apart from the Government of India Act of 1935. To that the Viceroy's reply, with the authority of His Majesty's Government, was sent to us on 23rd December. I had better quote it and not put it in my own words: "My answer to your first question is that the declaration I made with the approval of His Majesty's Government on October the 13th last does not exclude" – mark the words "does not exclude" – "examination of any part either of Act of 1935 or of the policy and plans on which it is based."

As regards other matters, we are still negotiating. The most important points are that no declaration should be made by His Majesty's Government with regard to the future Constitution of India without our approval and consent, and that no settlement of any question should be made with any party behind our back. Well, ladies and gentlemen, whether the British Government in their wisdom agree to give us that assurance or not, I trust that they will still see that it is a fair and just demand. We say that we cannot leave the future fate of 90 millions of people in the hands of anybody else. We, and we alone, must be the final arbiters of our destiny. Surely that is a just claim. We do not want that the British Government should thrust upon the Muslims a Constitution which they do not approve of and to which they do not agree. Therefore, the British Government will be well advised to give that assurance and give the Muslims complete peace and confidence in this matter and win their friendship. But whether they do that or not, after all as I have told you before, we must depend upon our own inherent strength. I make it plain from this platform that if any declaration is made, if any interim settlement is arrived at, without our approval and without our consent, the Muslims of India will resist it. And no mistake should be made on that score.

The next point is with regard to Palestine. We are told that "endeavours, earnest endeavours, are being made to meet the reasonable national demands of the Arabs". Well, we cannot be satisfied by earnest endeavours, sincere endeavours, best endeavours. We want that the British Government should in fact and actually meet the demands of the Arabs in Palestine.

Another point is with regard to the sending of the troops abroad. Here there is some misunderstanding. But anyhow we have made clear our position that we did not demand that Indian troops should not be used to the fullest for the defence of our country. Hence if there are any misapprehensions on this score they are not justified. We simply wanted the British Government to give us assurance that Indian troops would not be sent against any Muslim country or any Muslim Power. Let us hope that we may yet be able to get the British Government to clarify the situation further.

This, then, is the position with regard to the British Government. The last meeting of the Working Committee had asked the Viceroy to reconsider his letter of 23rd December, having regard to what had been explained to him in pursuance of the resolution of the Working Committee passed on 3rd February. We are informed that the matter is receiving his careful consideration.

Ladies and gentlemen, that is where we have stood since the outbreak of the war and up to 3rd February. As far as our internal position is concerned, we have been examining it. As you know, there are several schemes which have been proposed by various well-informed constitutionalists and others who take interest in the problem of India's future Constitution. We have also appointed a sub-committee to examine the details of the schemes that have come in so far. But one thing is quite clear. It has always been taken for granted mistakenly that the Muslims are a minority and, of course, we ourselves have got used to it for such a long time. Settled notions such as this one sometimes are very difficult to remove. The Muslims are not a minority. The Muslims are a nation by any definition. The British and, particularly, the Congress proceed on the basis, "Well, you are a minority after all, what do you want?" "What else do the minorities want?", as Babu Rajendra Prasad said. But surely the Muslims are not a minority. We find that even according to the British map of India, we occupy large parts of this country, where the Muslims are in a majority, such as Bengal, Punjab, NWFP, Sind and Baluchistan.

Now the question is, what is the best solution of this problem between the Hindus and the Muslims? We have been considering, and as I have already said, a committee has been appointed to consider the various proposals. But whatever the final scheme of Constitution, I will present to you my views and in confirmation of what I am going to put before you, I will just read to you a letter from Lala Lajpat Rai to Mr CR Das. It was written, I believe, about fourteen or fifteen years ago and that letter has been reproduced in a recently published book by one Indra Prakash, and that is how this letter has come to light. Lala Lajpat Rai was a very astute politician and a staunch Hindu Mahasabhite. But before I read this letter let me say that it is plain from it that you cannot get away from being a Hindu if you are a Hindu! The word 'nationalist' has now become the plaything of conjurers in politics. This is what he says:

"There is one point more which has been troubling me very much of late and one which I want you to think about carefully and that is the question of Hindu-Mohammedan unity. I have devoted most of my time during the last six months to the study of Muslim history and Muslim law and I am inclined to think it is neither possible nor practicable. Assuming and admitting the sincerity of Mohammedan leaders in the non-cooperation movement, I think their religion provides an effective bar to anything of the kind.

'You remember the conversation I reported to you in Calcutta which I had with Hakim Ajmal Khan and Dr Kitchlew. There is no finer Mohammedan in Hindustan than Hakim

Ajmal Khan, but can any Muslim leader override the Koran? I can only hope that my reading of the Islamic law is incorrect.' I think his reading is quite correct. And nothing would relieve me more than to be convinced that it is so. But if it is right then it comes to this that although we can unite against the British we cannot do so to rule Hindustan on British lines. We cannot do so to rule Hindustan on democratic lines."

Ladies and gentlemen, when Lala Lajpat Rai said that we cannot rule this country on democratic lines it was all right but when I had the temerity to speak the same truth about eighteen months ago there was a shower of attacks and criticism. But Lala Lajpat Rai said fifteen years ago that we cannot do so, viz., to rule Hindustan on democratic lines. What is the remedy? The remedy according to the Congress is to keep us in the minority and under their majority rule. Lala Lajpat Rai proceeds further:

"What is then the remedy? I am not afraid of the seven crore, of Muslims. But I think the seven crore, in Hindustan plus the armed hosts of Afghanistan, Central Asia, Arabia, Mesopotamia and Turkey, will be irresistible. I do honestly and sincerely believe in the necessity or desirability of Hindu-Muslim unity. I am also fully prepared to trust the Muslim leaders. But what about the injunctions of the Koran and Hadis? The leaders cannot override them. Are we then doomed? I hope your learned mind and wise head will find some way out of this difficulty."

Now, ladies and gentlemen, that is merely a letter written by one great Hindu leader to another great Hindu leader fifteen years ago. Now, I should like to put before you my views on the subject taking everything into consideration as it strikes me at the present moment. The British Government and Parliament, and indeed the British nation, have for many decades past been brought up and nurtured on settled notions about India's future. These notions are based on developments in their own country, which have resulted in the British Constitution, functioning through the Houses of Parliament and the cabinet system. Their concept of government by parties, functioning on the political plane, has become the ideal with them. They regard it as the best form of government for every country. The powerful one-sided propaganda of the Congress party, which naturally appeals to the British, has led them into a serious blunder – that of producing the Constitution envisaged in the Government of India Act of 1935. We find that most leading statesmen of Great Britain, saturated with these notions, have in their pronouncements, seriously asserted and expressed the hope that the passage of time will harmonise inconsistent elements in India.

A leading journal like the *London Times*, commenting on the Government of India Act of 1935, wrote, 'Undoubtedly the differences between the Hindus and Muslims are not of religion in the strict sense of the word but also of law and culture, that they may be said, indeed, to represent two entirely distinct and separate civilizations. However, in the course of time, the superstition will die out and India will be moulded into a single nation.' So, according to the *London Times,* the only difficulties are the superstitions. These fundamental and deep-rooted differences in the spiritual, economic, social and political spheres have been euphemised as mere 'superstitions'. But surely it is a flagrant disregard of the past history of the subcontinent of India, as well as of the fundamental Islamic conception of society vis-a-vis that of Hinduism, to characterise these differences as mere 'superstitions'.

Notwithstanding a thousand years of close contact, nationalities, which are as divergent today as ever, cannot at any time be expected to be transformed into one nation merely by the method of subjecting them to a democratic Constitution and holding them forcibly together by the unnatural and artificial means of a British Parliamentary statute. What the unitary government of India had failed to achieve in 150 years cannot be realised by the imposition of a central federal government. It is inconceivable that the fiat or the writ of a government so constituted can ever command willing and loyal obedience throughout the subcontinent by various nationalities, except by means of the armed force behind it.

The problem in India is not that of an inter-communal character but manifestly of an international one, and it must be treated as such. So long as this basic and fundamental truth is not realised, any Constitution that may be built will result in disaster and will prove destructive and harmful not only to the Muslims but also to the British and Hindus. If the British Government is really in earnest and sincere to secure peace and happiness for the people of this subcontinent, the only course open to them is to allow the major nations to have separate homelands by dividing India into autonomous national states. There is no reason why these states should be antagonistic to each other. On the contrary, the rivalry between them and the desire and effort on the part of one to dominate the social order and establish political supremacy over the other in the government of the country will disappear. It will lead more towards natural goodwill and, by international pacts between them, they can live in complete harmony as neighbours. This will lead further to a friendly settlement, all the more easily, with regard to minorities by reciprocal arrangements and adjustments between Muslim India and Hindu India, which will far more adequately and effectively safeguard the rights and interests of Muslims and various other minorities.

It is extremely difficult to appreciate why our Hindu friends fail to understand the real nature of Islam and Hinduism. They are not religions in the strict sense of the word, but are, in fact, different and distinct social orders. It is a dream that the Hindus and Muslims can ever evolve a common nationality, This notion of one Indian nation has gone far beyond the limits and is the cause of most of our troubles and will lead India to destruction if we fail to revise this misconception in time. The Hindus and Muslims have different religious philosophies, social customs and literatures. They neither intermarry nor inter-dine and, indeed, they belong to two different civilisations which are based mainly on conflicting ideas and conceptions. Their views on life and of life are different. It is also quite clear that Hindus and Muslims derive their inspiration from different sources of history. They have different epics, different heroes in different episodes. Very often the hero of one is a foe of the other and likewise, their victories and defeats overlap. To yoke together two such nations under a single state, one a numerical minority and the other a majority, must lead to growing discontent and the final destruction of any fabric that may be so built-up for the government of such a state.

History has presented to us many similar examples, such as the union of Great Britain and Ireland, of Czechoslovakia and Poland with Austria. History has also shown that many geographical tracts, much smaller than the subcontinent of India, which might otherwise have been called one country, have been divided into as many states as there are nations inhabiting them. The Balkan Peninsula comprises as many as seven or eight sovereign states. Likewise, the Portuguese and the Spanish stand divided in the Iberian Peninsula. Whereas, under the plea of the unity of India and one nation, which does not exist, it is sought to pursue the line of one central government. We know that the history of the last twelve hundred years has failed to achieve unity, and have witnessed, during the ages, India always divided into Hindu India and Muslim India. The present artificial unity of India dates back only to the British conquest and is maintained by British bayonets. The termination of the British regime, which is implicit in the recent declaration of His Majesty's Government, will be the herald of an entire break-up, and a worse disaster for the Muslims than has ever taken place during the last one thousand years. Surely that is not the legacy which Britain would bequeath to India after 150 years of her rule, nor would Hindu and Muslim India risk such a sure catastrophe.

Muslim India cannot accept any Constitution which must necessarily result in a Hindu majority government. If Hindus and Muslims are brought together under a democratic system, forced upon the minorities, it can only mean Hindu raj. Democracy of the kind with which the Congress High Command is enamoured would mean the complete destruction of what is most precious in Islam. We have had ample experience of the working of the provincial Constitutions during the last two and a half years. Any repetition of such government must lead to civil war and the raising of private armies, as was recommended by Mr Gandhi to the Hindus of Sukkur. He told them that they must defend themselves non-violently or violently, giving blow for blow, and if they could not, they must emigrate. Muslims are not a minority as it is commonly known and understood.

One has only to look around. Even today, according to the British map of India, in four out of eleven provinces, the Muslims predominate more or less. Here governments are functioning notwithstanding the decision of the Hindu Congress High Command to non-cooperate and prepare for civil disobedience. Muslims are a nation according to any definition of a nation, and they must have their homelands, their territory and their state. We wish to live in peace and harmony with our neighbours as a free and independent people. We wish to develop to the fullest our spiritual, cultural, economic, social and political life in a way that we think best and in consonance with our own ideal and according to the genius of our people. Honesty demands and the vital interest of millions of our people impose a sacred duty upon us to find an honourable and peaceful solution, which would be just and fair to all. But at the same time, we cannot be moved or diverted from our purpose and objective by threats or intimidation. We must be prepared to face all difficulties and make all the sacrifices that may be required of us to achieve the goal we have set in front of us.

Ladies and gentlemen, that is the task before us. I fear I have gone beyond my time limit. Still there are many other things that I should like to tell you, but I have already published a little pamphlet containing most of what I have to say. You could easily get that publication both in English and in Urdu from the League office. It might give you a clearer idea of our aims. It contains some very important resolutions of the Muslim League and various other statements. Anyhow, I have placed before you the task that lies ahead of us. Do you realise how big and stupendous it is? Do you realise that you cannot get freedom or independence by mere arguments? I want to appeal to the intelligentsia. The intelligentsia in all countries of the world has been the pioneer of movements for freedom. What does the Muslim intelligentsia propose to do? I tell you that unless you get this into your blood, unless you are prepared to take off your coats and are willing to make sacrifices and work selflessly, earnestly and sincerely for your people, you will never realise your aim. Friends, I therefore want you to make up your mind definitely and then think of devices to strengthen your organisation and consolidate the Muslims all over India. I think that the masses are wide awake. They only want your guidance and your lead. Come forward as servants of Islam, organise the people economically, socially, educationally and politically and I am sure that you will be a power that will be recognized by everybody.

Pakistan Resolution 23 March 1940

THE ALL India Muslim League held its session in Lahore on 23 March 1940, in which the famous Lahore Resolution (now called the 'Pakistan Resolution') was adopted. The Resolution runs as under:

> Resolved that it is the considered view of this session of the All India Muslim League that no Constitutional Plan would be workable in this country or acceptable to Muslims, unless it is designed on the following basic principle, namely, the geographically contiguous units are demarcated into regions which should be so constituted, with such territorial readjustments as may be necessary, that the areas in which the Muslims are numerically in a majority as in the North Western and Eastern Zones of India, should be grouped to constitute 'independent states', in which the constituent units shall be autonomous and sovereign.

That adequate, effective, and mandatory safeguards should be specifically provided in the constitution for minorities in these units and in these regions for the protection of their religious, cultural, economic, political, administrative, and other rights and interests in consultation with them. And in other parts of India, where the Mussalmans are in a minority, adequate, effective, and mandatory safeguards shall be specially provided in the constitution for them and other minorities for the protection of their religious, cultural, economic, political, administrative, and other rights and interests in consultation with them.

This session further authorizes the Working Committee to frame a scheme of constitution in accordance with these basic principles providing for the assumption finally by the respective regions of all powers such as defence, external affairs, communications, customs, and such other matters as may be necessary.

Jinnah, in his famous address on the occasion, gave clear expression to the basic concept underlying the resolution. Some of the extracts from his address reproduced below:

It has always been taken for granted mistakenly that the Mussalmans are a minority. The Mussalmans are not a minority. The Mussalmans are a nation by any definition. What the military Government of India for 150 years has failed to achieve cannot be realized by the imposition of Central Federal Government except by means of armed force. The problem in India is not of an inter-communal character but manifestly of an international one and must be treated as such. The Hindus and Muslims belong to two different civilizations which are based mainly on conflicting ideas and conceptions. To yoke together two such nations under a single state, one as a numerical minority and the other as a majority, must lead to growing discontent and final destruction of any fabric that may be so built up for the government of such a state.

Tracts on Population Transfers

I

Ambedkar on Partition

THE MUSLIM League officially resolved to demand Partition on 23rd March 1940. Dr BR Ambedkar soon set about thinking through the ramifications of creating Pakistan. The author of this book has not come across anyone who thought so quickly, so thoroughly, or so sincerely about the security of Hindus. What he wrote gives an insight into what he thought of partition six or seven years before it took place. And how remarkably right he was. Had we listened to him, India would not have suffered.

By 1941, Dr Ambedkar's detailed work entitled *Pakistan or the Partition of India* was on the shelves of shops. By 1946, a third edition had been published. Much later in 1990, the book was reprinted as part of Ambedkar's complete works by the state government of Maharashtra. It formed Volume 8 of the comprehensive publication.

Dr Ambedkar was one of the few people who recommended partition for the sake of Hindu safety and Indian's military security. He, however insisted on the bifurcation of Bengal and Punjab, so that most Hindus of those provinces could stay in India without having to move or migrate. Apart from the inevitable vivisection of territory, he strongly advocated an exchange of population. The Muslims on the Indian side were to migrate to Pakistan and non-Muslims from Pakistani territory were to come away to this side of the border.

Dr Ambedkar did not consider the transfer of population unduly difficult and quoted the precedents of Bulgaria, Greece and Turkey.

How would the creation of Pakistan affect the defence of Hindustan? This question was posed by Babasaheb from the viewpoints of frontiers, of resources, of the armed forces, of communal peace, of redrawing of boundaries. The creation of Pakistan would leave Hindustan without a scientific frontier. There are two considerations, which, if taken into account, will show that the apprehensions of the Hindus in this matter are quite uncalled for. In the first place, can any country hope to have a frontier which may be called scientific? As Mr Davies, the author of *North-West Frontier* observes:

> "It would be impossible to demarcate on the North-West of our Indian Empire a frontier which would satisfy ethnological, political and military requirements.

To seek for a zone which traverses easily defineable geographical features; which does not violate ethnic considerations by cutting through the territories of closely related tribes; and which at the same time serves as a political boundary, is utopian."

As a matter of history, there has been no one scientific boundary for India and different persons have advocated different boundaries for India. The question of boundaries has given rise to two policies, the "forward policy" and the "back to the Indus policy". The forward policy had a greater and a lesser intent, to use the terminology of Sir George Macmunn, a senior British official. In its greater intent it meant active control of the affairs of Afghanistan and the extension of Indian influence up to the Oxus river. In its lesser intent, it was confined to the absorption of the tribal hills between the administered territory (i.e. the Province of North West Frontier) and Afghanistan as defined by the Durand Line and the exercise of British control right up to that line. The greater intent of the forward policy as a basis for a safe boundary for India has long been abandoned. Consequently, there remain three possible boundary lines to choose from (l) the Indus river (2) the present administrative boundary of the NWFP and (3) the Durand Line. Pakistan will no doubt bring the boundary of India back to the Indus, indeed, behind the Indus to the Sutlej. But this back to the Indus policy was not without its advocates. The greatest exponent of the Indus boundary was Lord Lawrence, a British expert who was vehemently opposed to any forward move beyond the trans-Indus foothills. He advocated meeting any invader in the valley of the Indus. In his opinion it would be an act of folly and weakness to give battle at any great distance from the Indus base; and the longer the distance an invading army has to march through Afghanistan and the tribal country, the more harassed it would be. Others no doubt have pointed out that a river is a weak line of defence. But the principal reason for not retiring to the Indus boundary seems to lie elsewhere. Mr Davies gives the real reason when he says that, '"The "Back to Indus" cry becomes absurd when it is examined from the point of view of the inhabitants of the modern North-West Frontier Province. Not only would withdrawal mean loss of prestige but it would also be a gross betrayal of those peoples to whom we have extended our beneficent rule."

In fact, it is no use insisting that any particular boundary is the safest, for the simple reason that geographical conditions are not decisive in the world today and modern technology has robbed natural frontiers of much of their former importance, even where there are mighty mountains, the broadest streams, widest seas or far stretching deserts.

In the second place, it is always possible for nations with no natural boundaries to make good this defect. Countries that have no natural boundaries are not wanting. Yet, all have made good the deficiencies of nature, by creating artificial fortifications as barriers, which can be far more impregnable than natural barriers. There is no reason to suppose that the Hindus will not be able to accomplish what other countries similarly situated have done. Given the resources, Hindus need have no fear for want of a naturally safe frontier.

More important than the question of a scientific frontier, is the factor of resources. If resources are ample for necessary equipment, then it is always possible to overcome the difficulties created by an unscientific or a weak frontier. We must, therefore, consider the comparative resources of Pakistan and Hindustan. The following figures are intended to convey an idea of their comparative position.

Resources of Pakistan*

Provinces	Area	Population	Revenues* Rs
NWFP	13.518	2.425.003	1.90.11.842
Punjab	91,919	23.551,210	12.53.87.730
Sind	46.378	3.887.070	9.56.76.269
Baluchistan	54.228	420.648	—
Bengal	82.955	50.000.000	36.55.62,485
Total	288.998	80,283,931	60,56,38,326

** Revenues include revenue raised both by provincial governments in the provinces from provincial sources and by the central government from central revenues.*

Resources of Hindustan*

Provinces	Area	Population	Revenues* Rs
Ajmer-Merwara	2.711	560.292	21.00.000
Assam	55.014	8.622.251	4,46.04,441
Bihar	69.348	32.371,434	6.78.21.588
Bombay	77.271	18.000.000	34.98.03.800
CP&Berar	99.957	15.507.723	4.58.83.962
Coorg	1.593	163.327	11.00.000
Delhi	573	636.246	70.00.000
Madras	142.277	46.000.000	25.66.71.265
Orissa	32.695	8.043.681	87.67.269
UP	206.248	48,408.763*	16.85.52.881
Total	607.657	178.513.919	96.24.05.206

** Pre-World War II figures*

These are gross figures. They are subject to certain additions and deductions. Revenues derived by the central government from the railways, currency and post and telegraphs are not included in these figures, as it is not possible to ascertain how much is raised from each province. When it is done, certain additions will have to be made to the figures under revenue. There can be no doubt that the share from these heads of revenue that will come to Hindustan, will be much larger than the share that will go to Pakistan. Most of the deductions will fall to the lot of Pakistan. As will be shown later, some portion of the Punjab will have to be excluded from the scheme of western Pakistan. Similarly, some portion of Bengal will have to be excluded from the proposed eastern Pakistan, although a district from Assam will have to be added to it. Thus, fifteen districts will have to be excluded from Bengal and thirteen from the Punjab. Sufficient data are not available to enable anyone to give an exact idea of what would be the reduction in the area, population and revenue, that would result from the exclusion of these districts. One may, however, hazard the guess that so far as Punjab and Bengal are concerned, their revenues would be halved. What is lost by Pakistan by this exclusion, will be gained by Hindustan. To put it in concrete terms, while the revenues of western and eastern Pakistan will be Rs 60 crore minus 24 crore or a nett Rs 36 crore, the revenues of Hindustan will be about 96 crore, plus 24 crore or a total 120 crore.

The study of the figures, in the light of these observations will show that the resources of Hindustan are far greater than those of Pakistan, whether one considers the question in terms of area, population or revenue. There need, therefore, be no apprehension on the score of resources. The creation of Pakistan will not leave Hindustan in a weakened condition. The defence of a country does not depend so much upon its scientific frontiers as it does upon its resources. But more than even the resources it depends upon the fighting forces available to it. What are the fighting forces available to Pakistan and to Hindustan?

The Simon Commission in 1930 pointed out, as a special feature of the Indian defence problem, that there were special areas which alone offered recruits to the Indian army and that there were other areas which offered none or, if at all, very few. The facts revealed in the following table, taken from the report of the Commission, undoubtedly will come as a surprise to many Indians, who think and care about the defence of India:

Areas of Recruitment	***Number of Recruits drawn***
1. North West Frontier Province	5,600
2. Kashmir	6,500
3. Punjab	86,000
4. Baluchistan	300
5. Nepal	19,000
6. United Provinces	16,500
7. Rajputana	7,000
8. Central India	200*
9. Bombay	7,000
10. Central Provinces + Berar	100
11. Bihar & Orissa	300

12.	Bengal	Nil
13.	Assam	Nil
14.	Burma	3,000
15.	Hyderabad	700
16.	Mysore	100
17.	Madras	4,000
18.	Miscellaneous	1,900
	Total	**158,200**

** Based on World War I Figures*

NB: This chapter and the following ones have been reproduced from Ambedkar: *Pakistan or the Partition of India,* originally published in 1941 and reprinted by the Government of Maharashtra in 1990.

The Simon Commission found that this state of affairs was natural to India and in support of it cited the following figures of recruitment from the different provinces of India during World War I, especially because it cannot be suggested that any discouragement was offered for recruitment in any area:

Province	***Combatant Recruits Enlisted***	***Non-Combatant***	***Total***
Madras	51,223	41,117	92,340
Bombay	41,272	30,211	71,483
Bengal	7,117	51,935	59,052
United Provinces	163,578	117,565	281,143
Punjab	349,688	97,288	446,976
North-West Frontier	32,181	13,050	45,231
Baluchistan	1,761	327	2,088
Burma	14,094	4,579	18,673
Bihar & Orissa	8,576	32,976	41,552

Central Provinces	5,376	9,631	15,007
Assam	942	14,182	15,124
Ajmer-Mewar	7,341	1,632	8,973
Nepal	58,904	Nil	58,904
Total	**742,053**	**742,053**	**1,156,546**

These data reveal that the fighting forces available for the defence of India mostly come from areas which are to be included in Pakistan. From this it may be argued, that without Pakistan, Hindustan cannot defend itself.

The facts brought out by the Simon Commission are beyond question. But they cannot be made the basis of the conclusion that only Pakistan can produce soldiers and that Hindustan cannot. That such a conclusion is quite untenable as will be seen from the following considerations.

In the first place, what is regarded by the Commission as something peculiar to India is not quite so peculiar. What appears to be peculiar is not due to any inherent defect in the people. The peculiarity arises from the policy of recruitment followed by the British government in the years past. The official explanation of the predominance in the Indian army of the men of the North-West is that they belong to the martial classes. But Mr Chaudhari, a military expert, has demonstrated that this explanation is far from being true. He has shown that the predominance in the army of the men from the North-West took place as early as the Mutiny of 1857, some 20 years before the theory of martial and non-martial classes was projected in an indistinct form for the first time in 1879 by the Special

Army Committee, and that their predominance had nothing to do with their alleged fighting qualities but was due to the fact, that they helped the British to suppress the Mutiny in which the Bengal army was so completely involved.

Hindustan need, therefore, have no apprehension regarding the supply of an adequate fighting force from among its own people. The separation of Pakistan cannot weaken her in that respect.

The Simon Commission drew attention to three features of the Indian army, which struck them as being special and peculiar to India. It pointed out that the duty of the army in India was two-fold; first, to prevent independent tribes on the Indian side of the Afghan frontier from raiding peaceful inhabitants of the plans below. Second, to protect India against invasion by countries lying behind and beyond unorganized territories. The commission took note of the fact that from 1850 to 1922, there were 72 expeditions against independent tribes, on an average of one a year, and also of the fact that in the countries behind and beyond this belt of unorganized territory, lies the direction from which, throughout the ages, danger to India's territorial integrity has come. The second unique feature of the Indian army, the Commission observed:

The Army in India is not only provided and organized to ensure against external dangers of a wholly exceptional character: it is also distributed and habitually used throughout India for the purpose of maintaining or restoring internal peace. In all countries the military is not normally employed in this way, and certainly is not organized for this purpose. But the case of India is entirely different. Troops are employed many times a year to prevent internal disorder and if necessary to quell it. Police forces admirably organized as they are cannot be expected in all cases to cope with the sudden and violent outburst of a mob driven frantic by religious frenzy."

The third unique feature of the Indian army which was pointed out by the Commission, is the preponderance in it of the men from the North- West. The origin of this preponderance and the reasons underlying the official explanation given, have already been examined.

But there is one more special feature of the Indian army to which the Commission made no reference at all. The Commission either ignored the fourth special feature or was not aware of it. It is such an important feature that it overshadows all the three features to which the Commission refers, in its importance and in its social and political consequences. It is a feature which, if widely known, will set many people thinking furiously. It is sure to raise questions which may prove insoluble and which may easily block the path of India's political progress – questions of far greater importance and complexity than those relating to Indianisation of the army.

Yet another feature of the Indian army is the much overlooked question of communal composition. Mr Chaudhari has highlighted this aspect. The following table shows the proportion of soldiers serving in the Indian infantry, according to the area and the community from which they are drawn:

Changes in the Communal Composition of the Indian Army

Area and Communities	%age in 1914	%age in 1918	%age in 1919	%age 1930
I. The NWFP				
Punjab, and 47 Kashmir	46.5	46	58.5	Nil
Sikhs	19.2	17.4	15.4	13.58
- Punjabi	11.1	11.3	12.4	22.6
Musalmans	6.2	5.42	4.54	6.35
- Pathans				
II. Nepal, Kumaon, Garhwal	15	18.9	14.9	22.00
- Gurkhas	13.1	16.6	12.2	16.4
III. Upper India 22				
- UP Rajputs	22.7	25.5	11.0	2.55
- Hindustani	6.4	6.8	7.7	Nil
Musalmans	1.8	1.86	2.5	
- Brahmins				
IV. South India	16	11.9	12	
- Mahrattas	4.9	3.85	3.7	5.5
- Madrasi	3.5	2.71	2.13	Nil
Musalmans	2.5	2.00	1.67	Nil
- Tamils				

The table brings out in an unmistakable manner the profound changes which have been going on in the communal composition of the Indian army particularly after 1919. They are (1) a phenomenal rise in the strengths of Punjabi Mussalmans and Pathans (2) a substantial reduction in the position of Sikhs from first to third, (3) the degradation of Rajputs to the fourth place, and (4) the shutting out of UP Brahmins, Madrasi Mussalmans, and Tamilians, both Brahmins and non-Brahmins.

Whatever be the explanation, two glaring facts stand out from this survey. The first is that the Indian army is predominantly Muslim in its composition. The other is that

Mussalmans who predominate are from the Punjab and the NWFP. Such a composition means that the Mussalmans have been made the principal defenders of India from foreign invasion. And they are conscious of this proud position which has been assigned to them by the British. One often hears them say that they are the gate-keepers of India. The Hindus must consider the problem of the defence of India in this light.

How far can the Hindus depend upon these gatekeepers to hold the gate and protect the liberty and freedom of India? The answer must depend on who comes to force open the gate. It is obvious that there are only two foreign countries which are likely to force this gate from the northwest side of India, Russia or Afghanistan—borders of both of them touch the borders of India. Which of them will invade India and when, no one can say definitely. If the invasion comes from Russia, it is hoped that the gate-keepers of India will be staunch and loyal enough to hold the gate and stop the invader. But suppose the Afghans singly or in combination with other Muslim countries march on India, will these gatekeepers stop the invaders or will they open the gates and let them in? This is a question which no Hindu can afford to ignore.

It is possible to say that Afghanistan will never think of invading India. But theory is best tested by examining its capacity to meet the worst-case scenario. The loyalty and dependability of the army of the Punjabi and North West Frontier Provinces Muslims can only be tested by considering how it will behave in the event of an invasion by the Afghans.

Will they respond to the call of the land of their birth, or, will they be swayed by the call of their religion, is the question which must be faced. It is not safe to try and escape from these annoying and discomfiting questions by believing that we need not worry about a foreign invasion so long as India is under the protection of the British. Such a complacent attitude is unforgivable. The last war has shown that a situation may arise when Great Britain may not be able to protect India, although it is in times of war when India needs the most protection.

Second, the efficiency of an institution must be tested under natural and not artificial conditions. The behaviour of the Indian soldier under British control is artificial. His behaviour when he is under Indian control would be his natural behaviour. British control does not allow much play to the natural instincts and sympathies of men. That is why the men in the army behave so well.

Some may ask: why assume that the large proportion of Muslims in the army is a settled fact and that it cannot be unsettled? Those who can unsettle it are welcome to make whatever efforts they can. But so far as one can see, it is not going to be unsettled. On the contrary, it should be no surprise if it was entered in the Constitution, when revised, as a safeguard for the Muslim minority. The Mussalmans are sure to make this demand and as against the Hindus, the Muslims somehow always succeed. We must, therefore, proceed on the assumption that the composition of the Indian army will remain at what it is at present. Can the Hindus depend on such an army to defend the country against invasion by Afghanistan? The realist must take note of the fact that Mussalmans look upon Hindus as kafirs, who deserve to be exterminated rather than protected. The realist must take note of the fact that while Mussalmans accept the European as his superior, he looks upon the Hindu as his inferior. It is doubtful how far a regiment of Mussalmans will accept the authority of Hindu officers if it be placed under them. The realist must take note that of all the Mussalmans, the ones from the North-West are the most disaffected in their relations with Hindus. The realist must take note that the Punjabi Mussalmans is fully susceptible to the propaganda in favour of pan-Islamism. Even Sir Theodore Morrison, writing in the Imperial Rule in India in 1899, was of the opinion that:

> "The views held by the Mohammedans (certainly the most aggressive and truculent of the peoples of India) are alone sufficient to prevent the establishment of an independent Indian Government. Were the Afghan to descend from the north upon an autonomous India, the Mohammedans, instead of uniting with the Sikhs and the Hindus to repel him, would be drawn by all the ties of kinship and religion to join his flag."

In 1919, Indian Mussalmans, who were carrying on the Khilafat movement, went as far as inviting the Amir of Afghanistan to invade India, and therefore the view expressed by Morrison acquires added strength and ceases to be a matter of mere speculation. There is another question which must be pondered by the Hindus. That question is: will the Indian government be free to use the army, whatever its loyalties, against the invading Afghans? Attention must be drawn to the stand taken by the Muslim League. It is to the effect that the Indian army shall not be used against Muslim powers. This principle was enunciated by the Khilafat Committee long before the League. Apart from this, the question remains: how far will the Indian Muslims, in future, make it their article of faith? That the League has not succeeded in this behalf against the British regime does not mean that it will not succeed against an Indian government. The chances are that it will, because, however unpatriotic the principle may be from the standpoint of Hindus, it is most agreeable to the Muslim sentiment, and the League may find sanction for it in the general support of its community. If the League succeeds in enforcing this limitation upon India's right to use her fighting forces, what is going to be the position of Hindus?

If India remains politically whole and the two-nation mentality created by Pakistan continues to be fostered, the Hindus will find themselves between the devil and the deep sea, so far as the defence of India is concerned. Having an army, they will not be free to use it because of the League's objections. Using it will not be possible nor depending on it, because its loyalty is doubtful. On account of these military limitations, India will have to remain on subordinate terms while cooperating with Muslim countries on her border, as do Indian states under British paramountcy.

Hindus have a difficult choice to make: to have a safe army

or a safe border? Is it in their interest to insist that Muslim India should remain part of India so that they may have a safe border, or is it in their interest to welcome its separation from India so that they may have a safe army? Which is then better for the Hindus? Should the Mussalmans be without and against or should they be within and against? If the question is asked of any prudent man, there will be only one answer, namely, that if the Mussalmans are to be against the Hindus, it is better that they should be without and against, rather than within and against. Indeed, it is a consummation devoutly to be wished that the Muslims should be without. That is the only way of getting rid of the Muslim preponderance in the Indian army.

How can it be brought about? Here again, there is only one way to bring it about and that is to support the scheme for creating Pakistan. Once Pakistan is created, Hindustan, having ample resources of men and money, can have an army which it can call its own and there will be nobody to dictate as to how it should be used and against whom it should be used. The defence of Hindustan, far from being weakened by the creation of Pakistan, will be infinitely improved.

The Pakistan area, which is the main recruiting ground of the present Indian army, contributes very little to the central exchequer as will be seen from the following figures:

As against this, the provinces of Hindustan contribute as follows:

Contribution to the Central Exchequer*

	Rs
Punjab	1,18,01,385
North-West Frontier	9,28,294
Sind	5,86,46,915
Baluchistan	Nil
Total	**7,13,76,594**
As against the above, the provinces of Hindustan contribute as follows:	
	Rs
Madras	9,53,26,745
Bombay	22,53,44,247
Bengal	12,00,00,000
UP	4,05,53,000
Bihar	1,54,37,742
CP & Berar	31,42,682
Assam	1,87,55,967
Orissa	5,67,346
Total	**51,91,27,729**

**Pre- World War II Figures*

Only 50% revenue is shown because nearly l/ 2 the population is Hindu.

The Pakistan provinces, it will be seen, contribute very little. The main contribution comes from the provinces of Hindustan. In fact, it is the money contributed by the provinces of Hindustan which enables the Government of India to carry out its activities in Pakistan provinces. The latter are a drain on the former. Not only do they contribute very little to the central government instead they receive a great deal from the centre. The revenue of the central government amounts to

Rs 121 crore, of this about Rs 52 crore, are spent annually on the army. In what area is this amount spent? Who pays the bulk of this amount of Rs 52 crore,? The bulk of this amount of (Rs 52 crore,) is spent on the Muslim army drawn from the Pakistan area. Now the bulk of this amount of (Rs 52 crore,) is contributed by Hindu provinces and is spent on an army which consists mainly of non-Hindus! How many Hindus are aware of this tragedy? How many know at whose cost this tragedy is being enacted? Today the Hindus are not responsible because they cannot prevent it. The question is whether they will allow this tragedy to continue. If they mean to stop it, the surest way of putting an end to it is to allow a Pakistan to come into being. To oppose it is to buy a sure weapon for their own destruction.

II

Pakistan and Communal Peace

Does Pakistan solve the communal question? A correct answer to this question calls for a close analysis of what is involved. One must have a clear idea as to what is meant exactly, when the Hindus and Muslims speak of the communal question.

It is not generally known that the communal question like the Forward policy for the frontier has a greater and a lesser intent and that in its lesser intent it means one thing, and in its greater intent it means a very different thing.

To begin with, the communal question in its lesser intent relates to the representation of Hindus and Muslims in the legislatures. Used in this sense, the question involves the settlement of two distinct problems:

> The number of seats to be allotted to Hindus and Muslims in different legislatures and the nature of the electorates through which these seats are to be filled.

The Muslims at the Round Table Conference claimed that their representatives from the entire provincial as well as the central legislatures should be elected by separate electorates, and they should be allowed to retain the weight-age in representation given to the Muslims in those provinces in which they were a minority in the population. In addition, they should be given a guaranteed majority of seats in the majority provinces such as the Punjab.

The Hindus from the beginning objected to both these demands. They insisted on joint electorates in all elections to all the legislatures, central and provincial, based on population ratio of representation.

The Communal Award of His Majesty's government settled this dispute by the simple, rough and ready method of giving the Muslims all that they wanted, without caring for Hindu opposition. The Award allowed the Muslims to retain weight-age and separate electorates, and in addition, gave them the statutory majority of seats in those provinces where they were in a majority of the population.

What is it in the Award that can be said to constitute a problem? Is there any force in the objections of the Hindus to the Communal Award? Whatever may be the correct measure of allotting representation to minorities, the Hindus cannot very well object to the weightage given to Muslim minorities, because similar wetghtage has been given to the Hindus in those provinces in which they are a minority. The treatment of Hindu minorities in Sind and the North West Frontier Province is a case in point.

Second, as to their objection to a statutory majority, it does not appear to be well founded. A system of guaranteed representation may be wrong and vicious and quite unjustifiable on theoretical and philosophical grounds. However, considered in the light of the circumstances, such as those obtaining in India, the system of statutory majority appears to be inevitable. Once it is granted that the representation given to a minority must not reduce the majority to minority, that very provision creates, as a mere counterpart, a system of statutory majority to the majority community. For fixing the seats of the minority involves the fixation of the seats of the majority. There is, therefore, no escape from the system of statutory majority, once it is conceded that the minority is not entitled to representation which would convert a majority into a minority.

There is, therefore, no great force in the objections of the Hindus to a statutory majority of Muslims in Punjab, the North West Frontier Province, Sind and Bengal. For, even in the provinces where the Hindus are in a majority and the Muslims in minority, the Hindus have got a statutory majority over the Muslims. At any rate, there is a parity of position and to that extent there can be no grounds for complaint. This does not mean that the objections set forth by Hindus have no substance and that there are no real grounds for opposing the Communal Award.

Muslim minorities in Hindu provinces insisted on separate electorates. This is really what it comes to when one remembers the usual position taken, viz. That the Muslim minorities cannot be deprived of their separate electorates without their consent, and the majority community of Hindus has been made to abide by their determination. Hindu minorities in Muslim provinces insisted that there should be joint electorates. Instead of conceding their claim, the Communal Award forced on them the system of separate electorates to which they objected. If in Hindu provinces, Muslim minorities are allowed the right of self-determination in the matter of electorates, the question arises: why are the Hindu minorities in the Muslim provinces not given the right of self-determination in the matter of their electorates? What is the answer to this question? And, if there is no answer, there is undoubtedly a deep seated inequity in the Award of His Majesty's government, which calls for redress.

To turn to the communal question in its greater intent: what is the problem, the Hindus ask? In its greater intent the communal question relates to the deliberate creation of Muslim provinces. Before the Act of 1935, there were only three provinces in which Muslims were in a majority in the Punjab, Bengal and the North West Frontier Province. The Muslims desired that the number of Muslim provinces be increased. With this objective in view, they demanded that Sind should be separated from Bombay Presidency and created into a new self governing province, and the North West Frontier should be raised to the status of a self-governing province. Neither

Sind nor the North West Frontier Province was financially self supporting. But in order to satisfy Muslim demand, the British government went as far as accepting the responsibility of giving an annual subvention to these provinces from central revenues.

The four provinces with Muslims in majority, now functioning as autonomous and self governing, were not created for administrative convenience nor for purposes of architectural symmetry: Hindu provinces poised against Muslim provinces. It is also true that the scheme of Muslim provinces was not a matter of satisfying Muslim pride. Asked what could be the purpose of having Muslim political power mobilized in this fashion, the Hindus answer that it was done to place in the hands of Muslims an effective weapon in their majority provinces to tyrannize the Hindu minorities, in case Muslim minorities in Hindu provinces were tyrannized by the Hindu majorities. The scheme thus became a system of protection, in which blast was to be met by counter-blast, terror by terror and tyranny by tyranny. The plan is undoubtedly a dreadful one, involving the maintenance of justice and peace by retaliation, and providing an opportunity for the punishment of an innocent minority,Hindus in Muslim provinces and Muslims in Hindu provinces, for the sins of their co-religionists in other provinces. It is a scheme of communal peace through a system of communal hostages.

The Muslims were aware from the start that the system of communal provinces was capable of being worked in this manner. It is clear from the speech made by Maulana Abul

Kalam Azad as President of the Muslim League session held in Calcutta in 1927. In his speech the Maulana declared:

> That by the Lucknow Pact they had sold away their interests. The Delhi proposals of March last opened the door for the first time to the recognition of the real rights of Musalmans in India. The separate electorates granted by the Pact of 1916 only ensured Muslim representation, but what was vital for the existence of the community was the recognition of its numerical strength. Delhi opened the way to the creation of such a state of affairs as would guarantee to them in the future of India a proper share. Their existing small majority in Bengal and the Punjab was only a census figure, but the Delhi proposals gave them for the first time five provinces of which no less than three (Sind: the Frontier Province and Baluchistan) contained a real overwhelming Muslim majority. If the Muslims did not recognise this great step they were not fit to live. There would now be nine Hindu provinces against five Muslim provinces, and whatever treatment Hindus accorded in the nine provinces. Muslims would accord the same treatment to Hindus in the five provinces. Was not this a great gain? Was not a new weapon gained for the assertion of Muslim rights?

III

Implications of Partition

How far does Pakistan approximate to the solution of the communal question? If the boundaries of Pakistan are to follow the present boundaries of the provinces in the north-west and in Bengal, it certainly does not eradicate the evils which lie at the heart of the communal question. It retains the very elements which give rise to it, namely, the pitting of a minority against a majority.

The rule over Hindu minorities by the Muslim majorities and the rule of the Muslim minorities by Hindu majorities are the crying evils of the present situation. This very evil will reproduce itself in Pakistan, if the provinces marked out for it are incorporated into it as they are, i.e. with boundaries drawn as at present.

Besides this, the evil which gives rise to the communal question in its larger intent, will not only persist as it is, but will assume a new malignancy. Under the existing system, the power centred in the communal provinces to do mischief to their hostages is limited by the power which the central government has over the provincial governments. At present, the hostages are at least within the pale of a central government which is Hindu in its composition and which has power to interfere for their protection.

But, when Pakistan becomes a Muslim state with full sovereignty over internal and external affairs, it would be free from the control of the central government. The Hindu minorities will have no recourse to an outside authority with overriding powers, to interfere on their behalf and curb this power of mischief, as under the scheme, no such overriding authority is permitted to exist. So, the position of Hindus in Pakistan may easily become similar to the condition of Armenians under the Turks or of Jews in Tsarist Russia or in Nazi Germany. Such a scheme would be intolerable and Hindus may well say that they cannot agree to Pakistan and leave their co-religionists as a helpless prey to the fanaticism of a Muslim national state.

This is a very frank statement of the consequences which will flow from giving effect to the creation of Pakistan. But care must be taken to locate the source of these consequences. Do they flow from the creation of Pakistan, or do they flow from particular boundaries that may be fixed for it? If the evils flow from the creation itself, if they are inherent, it is unnecessary for any Hindu to waste his time in considering it. He will be justified in summarily dismissing it. On the other hand, if the evils are the result of the boundaries, the question of Pakistan reduces itself to a mere question of changing the boundaries.

A study of the question amply supports the view that the evils of Pakistan are not inherent. If any evil results follow, they will have to be attributed to its boundaries. This becomes clear if one studies the distribution of population. The reasons why these evils will be reproduced within western and eastern Pakistan is because, with the present boundaries, they do not become single ethnic states. They remain mixed states, composed of a Muslim majority and a Hindu minority as before. The evils are the evils which are inseparable from a mixed state. If Pakistan is made a *single unified ethnic state*, the evils will automatically vanish. There will be no question of separate electorates within Pakistan, because in such a homogeneous Pakistan, there will be no majorities to rule and no minorities to be protected. Similarly, there will be no majority of one community holding in its possession, a minority of an opposing community.

The question, therefore, is one of demarcation of boundaries and reduces itself to: is it possible for the boundaries of Pakistan to be so fixed, that instead of producing a mixed state composed of majorities and minorities, with all the attendant evils, Pakistan will be an ethnic state composed of one homogeneous community, namely Muslims? The answer is that in a large part of the area affected by the project of the

League, a homogeneous state can be created by merely shifting the boundaries, and in the rest, homogeneity can be produced by shifting only the population.

Some scoff at the idea of shifting and exchange of population. But those who scoff can hardly be aware of the complications, which a minority problem gives rise to, and the attendant failures on almost all the efforts made to protect them. The constitutions of post-war states, as well as of older states in Europe which had a minority problem, proceeded on the assumption that constitutional safeguards for minorities should suffice for their protection, and therefore the constitutions of most of the new states with majorities and minorities were studded with long lists of fundamental rights and safeguards to see that they were not violated by the majorities. What has been the experience?

That the transfer of minorities is the only lasting remedy for communal peace is beyond doubt. If that is so, there is no reason why Hindus and Muslims should keep on trading in safeguards which have proved so unsafe. If small countries, with limited resources like Greece, Turkey and Bulgaria, were capable of such an undertaking, there is no reason to suppose that, what they did, cannot be accomplished by Indians. After all, the population involved is inconsiderable and because some obstacles require to be removed, it would be the height of folly to give up so sure a way to communal peace.

How far does the creation of Pakistan remove the communal question from Hindustan? That is a very legitimate question and must be considered. It must be admitted that by the creation of Pakistan, Hindustan is not freed of the communal question. While Pakistan can be made a homogeneous state by redrawing its boundaries, Hindustan must remain a composite state. Musalmans are scattered all over Hindustan, though they are mostly congregated in towns, and no ingenuity in the matter of redrawing of boundaries can make it homogeneous. *The only way to make Hindustan homogeneous is to arrange for exchange of population.* Until that is done, it must be admitted even with the creation of Pakistan, the problem of majority versus minority will remain in Hindustan as before and will continue to produce disharmony in the body politic of Hindustan.

Admitting that Pakistan is not capable of providing a complete solution to the communal problem within Hindustan, does it follow that the Hindus on that account should reject Pakistan? Before the Hindus draw any such hasty conclusion, they should consider the following effects of Pakistan.

First, consider the effect of Pakistan on the magnitude of the communal problem. That can be best gauged by reference to the Muslim population as it will be grouped within Pakistan and Hindustan.

These figures indicate that the Muslims who will be left in British Hindustan will be only 18,545,465 and the rest 47,897,301, forming a vast majority of the total Muslim population, will be out of it and will be the subjects of Pakistan. This distribution of the Muslim population, in terms of the communal problem, means that while without Pakistan the

Muslim Population in Pakistan*		**Muslim Population in Hindustan**	
1 Punjab	13,332,4601.	Total Muslim Population in British India (excluding Burma and Aden)	66,442,766
2. NWFP	2,227,303		
3. Sind	2,830,800		
4. Baluchistan	405,309		
5. Eastern Bengal Muslim States (i) Eastern Bengal (ii) Sylhet	 27,497,624 1,603,805 47,897,3013	2. Muslim Population grouped in Pakistan and Eastern Bengal State	47,897,301
		3. Balance of Muslims in British Hindustan	18,545,465

**Estimated by Ambedkar*

communal problem in India involves 6,5 crore, Muslims, with the creation of Pakistan it will involve only 2 crore. Is this to be of no consideration for Hindus who want communal peace? It seems that if Pakistan does not solve the communal problem within Hindustan, it substantially reduces it, becomes of minor significance and therefore much easier of peaceful solution.

These are the material advantages of Pakistan. There is another which is psychological. The Muslims, in southern and central India, draw their inspiration from the Muslims of the north and the east. If after the creation of Pakistan there is communal peace in the north and the east, as there should be, there being no majorities and minorities there, the Hindus may reasonably expect communal peace in Hindustan. This severance of the bond between the Muslims of the north and the east and the Muslims of Hindustan is another gain to the Hindus of Hindustan.

Taking into consideration these effects of Pakistan, it cannot be disputed that if Pakistan does not wholly solve the communal problem within Hindustan, it frees Hindus from the turbulence because of Muslims being predominant partners. It is for the Hindus to say whether they will reject such a proposal, simply because it does not offer a complete solution. Some gain is better than much harm.

IV

Brother Ahmed Ali Jinnah

When a Pakistani President addresses his nation on television, he has in the background the national flag as well as a portrait of Mohammed Ali Jinnah. He usually repeats that his country is an Islamic republic and in between swears by Allah. The glaring incongruity in the scene is the portrait of the *Qaid-e-Azam* or the founder of Pakistan who however was a Muslim only in name. He began life as Mohammed Ali Jinnahbhai. The suffix 'bhai' in his last name was dropped after his arrival in England. As Dr SM Ikram, in his work entitled *Modern Muslim India and The Birth of Pakistan*, Renaissance Publishing House, Delhi, 1991, has written that he was *"probably the first member of his family to have a distinctly Muslim name."*

His father's name was Jinnahbhai Poonja. His mother was

called Mithi Bai which in English would mean sweet lady. His grandfather was a Hindu Lohana with the first name Jinnahbhai, or tiny brother who was converted to an *Ismaili khoja*. The chief Ismaili religious book was *Dasavatar* or ten incarnations, so much a part of the Hindu ethos. In the words of Professor Asaf AA Fyzee, *Outlines of Muhammadan Law*, Oxford University Press, Delhi, 1999, the *original faith of the Ismaili khoja was a hybrid between Hinduism and Islam*. It is not uncommon to come across khoja families where the menfolk go to masjids but their women do *swaminarayan puja*. Names like Rambhai are also not unknown.

Ahmed Ali was the Qaid's younger brother and a friend of the author's grandfather, the late Dharam Das Vora of 401 Girgaum Road, Bombay 2. By 1946, Ahmed used to make fun of himself by claiming to be the prince of Pakistan. Although he said, he got an allowance of Rs. 600 per month from his brother, he often sounded endearingly envious of the Qaid. He looked so similar to his brother that he could be mistaken as his double. He often told his friend Vora that there was nothing wrong in enjoying a sundowner. Alcohol might be *haraam* for a Muslim but his family was not strictly Islamic. After all, the Jinnah's grandfather was a Hindu to begin with. He himself had married a Swiss lady who along with their daughter had gone back to Switzerland a little before World War II began.

The elder brother was more of a brown Englishman than either an Indian or a Muslim. He loved European clothes, especially those tailored in London, and seldom dressed in anything else, until after becoming the head of the Muslim League. He also liked a sundowner and had no objection to consuming any form of meat, whether *halal* or *jhatka*, whether beef or pork or mutton. This is confirmed by Justice MC Chagla, in his book *Roses in December*, Bharatiya Vidya Bhavan, 1973. He had long forgotten his Arabic, did not know how to offer namaz and never bothered to learn Urdu, brother Ahmed had added.

He told Vora that Mohammed Ali had no particular preference for the Muslim over the Hindu. He enjoyed socialising with the British as well as Westernised Indians, many of whom were Parsees in those days in Bombay. It so happened that his wife was a Parsee and so was his son-in-law Neville Wadia. He had little empathy with the masses and religion did not matter a great deal in the lives of the elite. Above all, his driving desire was to be a number one or *numero uno*, no matter where he was and what he was doing. This is confirmed by Justice Chagla in the words: *Jinnah's besetting fault was his obsessive egoism.*

In Ahmed's own words, his brother's one burning ambition was to be a *badshah*. This view was confirmed immediately on the birth of Pakistan. Jinnah declared that he was the Governor-General and the Prime Minister would do what he tells him to do. In line with India's invitation to Lord Mountbatten to continue to be its Governor-General, he had expected Pakistan to also invite him to be its titular head. But Jinnah had to be supreme and could not be reporting to anyone else. Read page 88 of the *Constitutional and Political History of Pakistan* by Hamid Khan, Oxford University Press, Karachi, 2001. The British journalist Beverly Nichols had described him in 1943 *as a potential emperor*.

In his early years, he had dreamt that one day he would rise to be the *badshah* of India. It was only when he found that this was an impractical prospect that Mohammed Ali plumped for becoming the sultan of a part of India. What happened to which Muslim and which Hindu as a result of the partition of India was purely incidental for him. Pakistan was merely a means to an end, which was his place in history as the founder of a state.

Who would know better than Jinnah that, for businessmen, that the creation of Pakistan was the opening up of an opportunity. As a *khoja* as well as a member of Bombay's elite, the Muslims he came in the closest contact with, were the *Khoja,* the *Memon* and the *Borah* commercial magnates. Although they were natural traders, they had to compete with the equally talented businessmen of other communities. For example, the Parsees had demonstrated considerable acumen at enterprise. The Gujarati *banias* had their areas of competence, especially in trading. Although the Marwaris did not dominate Bombay business, they certainly were recognised as a business factor to be reckoned with. As one moved out of Bombay towards north and eastern India, Marwari domination could be seen. South India was the playing field of the Chettiars, they were the champions. The *Khojas* and the *Memons* would have to continue to compete with all of these people in an undivided India. Whereas if there were a Pakistan, and they were to emigrate there, they might well enjoy near monopoly.

Some relatives of the author operated their oilseeds trading under the name and style of R Ratilal & Company. Ratilal Gandhi was the senior partner. He also happened to be an active Congressman and, for a few years, was the President of the Bombay Provincial Congress Committee. R Ratilal & Co were partners of the big house of Habibs, now remembered in India through the Habib Bank. In those days, all their business and investments were Bombay based. What was then the sense in Habibs financing the Muslim League, whose agenda was the creation of Pakistan? On being questioned by Ratilal as to the motive, one of the Habib brothers promptly replied:

> *We always have thought you to be a shrewd bania. Why then don't you see the enormous advantage the khojas and memons would have doing business in competition with the Punjabi farmers as distinct from the Hindu and Parsee entrepreneurs?*

It is impossible to accept that Jinnah was unaware of the intentions that led his wealthy supporters to finance his movement.

The author, in May 1961, happened to be on a voyage by a Lloyd Triestino steamer named *Victoria*, and one of his fellow passengers was Maqsood Ahmed, a grandson of the legendry Sir Syed Ahmad Khan of Aligarh fame. In the course of several conversations, a great deal was discussed. Ahmed was nostalgic about his years with the Imperial Tobacco Company headquartered in Calcutta. When Partition took place, Maqsood was a young executive. According to his calculation, by 1961, he could have been no. 5 in the company. Whereas, at the end of that voyage, he was to take over as the Chief Executive or the head of the Pakistan Tobacco Company whose mother corporation was the same as that of the Imperial or today's ITC Limited.

Surely, migration to Pakistan made so much sense for his career. Maqsood was candid enough to say that for the professional classes, the emergence of Pakistan was a godsend. Deputy Secretaries overnight became additional secretaries in the government. Majors became brigadiers. And so on. Any member of the Muslim elite who could migrate was assured of a better career. Only those who depended on agriculture and were insufficiently educated had a vested interest in staying put and therefore remaining in Hindustan. For the *ulema*, Pakistan meant the bifurcation of the Indian *ummah*.

*The judgement given by Justice J Amould of the Bombay High Court in a matter popularly known as Aga Khan case confirmed the reason for concealment. To quote, takiah or concealment of their religious views and adoption of aline (alien) religious ceremonies out of dread of persecution for religion sake (12 Born HCR 323-363).**

If the Qaid-e-Azam had lived on he would have been disappointed. In 1953, there were riots against the Ahmediyas.

An official committee was soon appointed to investigate the causes of the disturbances. The Chief Justice of the Lahore High Court, Mr Muhammad Munir, was the president of the committee. The Deobandi *ulema* declared *all that Asna Ashari Shias were kafirs and murtad (apostates) for not believing in the Sahabiyyat of Hazrat Siddiqui*.*

---

* As Asaf AA Fyzee, in his book *Outlines of Muhammadan Law*, fourth edition, Oxford University. *The Memoirs of Aga Khan*, New York, 1954.

* Akbar and qazif (deniers of the status) of Hazrat, Aisha Siddiqa, page 121 of the *Constitutional and Political History of Pakistan* by Hamid Khan, Oxford University Press, Karachi, 2001.

V

Two Nation Theory

The two nation theory on which rested the demand for partition made by the Muslim League has never been thought through by the Hindus. It was developed on the basis of what an Indian student at Cambridge University called Choudhary Rahmat Ali wrote in 1933, in a pamphlet entitled *Now or Never Pakistan, Are We to Live or Perish Forever*? This was written only seven years before Mohammed Ali Jinnah called for a separate Muslim homeland at the Lahore session of his party on 23 March 1940. Even during the intervening period, not much attention or debate had been devoted to analysing the dialectics of the two nation theory.

Nor was Choudhary Rahmat Ali, studying at Cambridge University in 1933, the author of this theory. *His credit is confined to innovating the name Pakistan. While presiding over the Allahabad session of the Muslim League in 1930, the famous poet Muhammad Iqbal had said that the Muslim demand for the creation of a Muslim India within India is, therefore, perfectly justified. The formation of a consolidated North-West Indian Muslim state appears to me to be the final destiny of the Muslims.*

Islam is a complete prescription. Religion, society, politics and life itself are all intertwined. Between the *Holy Quran* and the *Hadith*, there is an answer to every question. The only precondition is that the questioner must accept that the message contained in the Quran *Majeed* is final and that Muhammad Sahib was the last prophet. There can be no new revelation. This approach is easily understandable when one remembers that the Prophet was a versatile person who achieved success in all fields in which he took part. He might not have envisioned so comprehensively had he not been successful at once as a householder, a competent trader, a brave general, a capable king and a man of god.

Hinduism is very different. It is not a religion in the Judaic sense. It is an explanation of life at one end for the intellectual and, at the other, for a man of action, yet another for a simple person who seeks salvation through *bhakti* or devotion. Politics is far away from the Hindu explanation of life. If at all it has prescription for politics, it is confined to the worship of one's soil called *matribhoomi* or motherland. There is therefore, in contrast to Islam, attachment to territory.

Moving back to the 19th century, from 1887 Sir Syed Ahmad Khan of Aligarh Muslim University fame, had begun to stress that Hindus and Muslims constituted two separate nations in India.* Some years earlier, Prof Ameer Ali, who had founded the Central National Muhammedan Association in Calcutta, had expressed similar views, according to Aziz Ahmad.

The Qaid-e-Azam was an outstanding advocate as well as a political leader. He however laid no claims to being either an ideologue or a political scientist. In any case, an active politician seldom has the leisure to sit back, think and theorise. When asked the basis of his two nation theory, Jinnah's answer was rough and ready. The Muslims and Hindus were separate nations because their cultures, clothes, food habits, language and even their architecture were quite different. With so many differences, he saw no future in two distinct peoples living together in one country.

In any case, Jinnah, during the 1940s had repeatedly stated that Islam was in danger. Once the British left India, there could be no impartial government and the Hindu majority would, at best, ignore the Muslims and, at worst, oppress them. There was therefore no future for the Muslims in an undivided India. Hence, the demand rose for a separate homeland for the followers of Islam. He was also categorical in his demand that an *exchange*

---

* Page 265 of *Studies in Islamic Culture in the Indian Environment* by Prof Aziz Ahmad, Oxford University Press, 2000.

of population between Pakistan and Hindustan should be an integral part of the bifurcation. This meant that the Muslims, in what would remain of Hindustan, should migrate to Pakistan and non-Muslims living in the latter should move to Hindustan. This demand was not confined to the Qaid-e-Azam. Many other leaders of the party had not only supported the proposition but some of them had been more vehement in their expression, as recorded in the following paragraphs.

The well known Karachi daily, *Dawn,* extensively covered throughout 1946 what the League leaders demanded. At a press conference on 25 November, 1946, in Karachi, Jinnah appealed to the central as well as provincial governments to take up the question of population exchange.

Earlier that year, Sir Feroze Khan Noon who later rose to be Prime Minister of Pakistan, while addressing Muslim League legislators in Patna, had gone to the extent of threatening the re-enactment of the murderous orgies of Chengez Khan and Halaqu Khan if non-Muslims did not agree to the proposal for population transfer. Khan Iftikhar Hussain, the Nawab of Mamdot said that the exchange of population offered a practical solution for the problem of Muslims quoted in *Dawn,* 3 December. Pir Ilahi Bux, the Sindh leader, observed that he welcomed an exchange of population for the safety of the minorities, as it would put an end to all communal disturbances. Ismail Chundrigar, who also eventually became Prime Minister, said that the British had no right to hand over Muslims to a subject people, namely Hindus, over whom they had ruled for 500 years. Mohammad Ismail, a Madras leader, had declared that the Muslims of India were in the midst *of a jihad*. Shaukat Hayat Khan, son of the more famous Sir Sikander Hayat Khan, had also given out threats to support transfer of population.

Can a *momin* or a faithful be a nationalist? We need to take a look at the basic tenets of Islam. The Muslim is one who either accepts, resigns or submits to the will of Allah. Islam means acceptance, resignation or submission. In other words, some scholars say the *root* of the word is *tasleem*. While others prefer the word *Islama* which, according to the *Oxford History of Islam*, Oxford Univesity Press, New York, 1999, *means he gave up, surrendered or submitted*.

The religion has five basic pillars; the first of which is to openly proclaim that there is no God but Allah, Muhammad is a messenger of Allah. The second pillar is to pray or perform *namaz* five times a day. The third is to pay a tithe every year to religious officials. The amount has long been fixed as one-fortieth of one's annual income and liquid assets and the purpose was to use the money for the welfare of the poor. It is called *zakaat*. The fourth pillar of Islam is to observe a month long fast during the month of Ramadan. The fifth is to undertake Hajj or pilgrimage to Mecca.

What is especially unique about Islam is the belief that what *is good for the Muslims is meant to be good for all human beings regardless of religion, colour, or origin*. The dialectic of this belief is that it is the duty of the Muslim, or at least the Momin, to try and convert every non-believer to Islam for his own good. If he does not succeed, the threat of sword can be resorted to. Initially the only exceptions made were the people of the book, namely, the Jews, Christians and Sabeans who could be allowed to keep their religion provided they paid the *jaziya* or poll tax.

Subsequently, members of other faiths such as Hindus were also accepted as eligible for, what was called, the *dhimmi* or *zimmi* status.

Islam and nationalism in any form are two incompatible modes of thought and life. Sir Mohammad Iqbal, called it a contradiction in terms since Islam in its essence is above all conditions of time and space. Nationality with us is a pure idea; it has no geographical basis. But in as much as the average man demands a material centre of nationality, the Muslim looks for it in the holy town of Mecca.

Maulana Abul Kalam Azad, in his early years, edited a famous Urdu journal called *Al Hilal*. When someone asked him a question as to which political party should Indian Muslims join, Azad's reply was eloquent: *Mussalmans need not join any party. They are the ones who for centuries made the world join their party and follow their path. They constitute the Party of God or Hizbullah.* The paper called upon everyone not to put undue trust in the government or to take lessons from the Hindu. He pushed his argument to its logical conclusion when he wrote that a Muslim who was seeking sanction for any action or belief in any other political party or school of thought, ceased to be a Muslim and could be regarded as a political polytheist for seeking a solution alien to the all embracing doctrine of the Quran.

What comes through from Azad's writings is that Islam is a complete prescription. Religion, society, politics and life itself are all intertwined. Hinduism is very different. It is an explanation of life at one end for the intellectual or a *gyani* and at the other for a man of action or a *karmayogi*, yet another for a simple person who seeks salvation through bhakti or devotion. It is not difficult for a Hindu to be a nationalist. Nor has the Parsee or the Christian any problem. In fact, nationalism grew out of Christian Europe.

All these factors do justify Mohammed Ali Jinnah's contention that Muslims are different. To that extent, his separatist theory, which was the basis of Partition, was consistent although it was labelled as the two nation theory. Would not *Seperation of Momins from Kafirs Theory* be a more suitable name? Nevertheless, his insistence on a complete exchange of population was consistent with his separatist theory.

No matter what the nomenclature, Jinnah had developed deep conviction in separatism. A liberal nationalist had turned into a sectarian separatist. Whether the metamorphosis was genuine or mercenary is for the reader to analyse. There never arose a question with regard to his integrity; his public record as well as his private conduct was consistently honest. At the same time, there was no doubt that his ego was king size and his ambition was to be number one wherever he was. Jinnah's separatism and its logic as he saw it are best described in his own words. Since he wrote little, the interview taken in December 1943 by Beverly Nichols, a British journalist, is invaluable and deserves to be quoted *ad lib*.*

That the Qaid-e-Azam had not thought through his cause for a state would be obvious to the reader. The argument is rough and ready, incomplete if not superficial, which leads one to think that Jinnah was riding the crest of a mass Muslim wave rather than leading a movement for Pakistan. Was he not fulfilling a personal ambition rather than pursuing a historic mission?

> *SELF: The most common accusation of your critics is that you have not defined Pakistan with sufficient precision - that there are many details of defence, economics, minorities, etc., which you have left deliberately vague. Do you think that is a just criticism?*
>
> *JINNAH: It is neither just nor intelligent, particularly if it is made by an Englishman with any knowledge of his own history. When Ireland was separated from Britain, the document embodying the terms of the separation was approximately ten lines. Ten lines of print to settle a dispute of incredible complexity which has poisoned British politics for centuries! All the details were left to the Future – and the Future is often an admirable arbitrator. Well, I've already given the world a good deal more than ten lines to indicate the principles and practice of Pakistan, but it is beyond the power of any man to provide, in advance, a blueprint in which every detail is settled. Besides, Indian history proves*

* It appeared in a book called *A Verdict on India*, Jonathan Cape, London, 1944.

that such a blue-print is totally unnecessary. Where was the blue-print when the question of Burma's separation was decided at the Round Table Conference? Where was the blue-print when Sindh was separated from Bombay? The answer; of course, is nowhere. It didn't exist. It didn't need to exist. The vital point was that the principle of separation was accepted; the rest followed automatically.

SELF: How would you describe the 'vital principles' of Pakistan?

JINNAH: In five words. The Muslims are a Nation. If you grant that, and if you are an honest man, you must grant the principle of Pakistan. You would have to grant it even if the obstacles "were a hundred times more formidable than they actually are. Of course, if you do not grant it, then ... He shrugged his shoulders and smiled ... Then, there is an end of the matter.

SELF: When you say the Muslims are a Nation, are you thinking in terms oj religion?

JINNAH: Partly but by no means exclusively. You must remember that Islam is not merely a religious doctrine but a realistic and practical Code of Conduct. I am thinking in terms of life, of everything important in life. I am thinking in terms of our history, our heroes, our art, our architecture, our music, our laws, our jurisprudence...

SELF: Please, I would like to write these things down.

JINNAH: (after a pause) in all these things our outlook is not only fundamentally differenı but often radically antagonistic to the Hindus. We are different beings. There is nothing in life which links us together. Our names, our clothes, our foods – they are all different; our economic life, our educational ideas, our treatment of women, our attitude to animals. We challenge each other at every point of the compass. Take one example, the eternal question of the cow. We eat the cow, the Hindus worship it. A lot of Englishmen imagine that this 'worship' is merely a picturesque convention, a historical survival. It is nothing of the sort. Only a few days ago, in this very city, the cow question became a matter for the police. The Hindus were thrown into the greatest agitation because cows were being killed in public. But the cow question is only one of a thousand. (A pause) What have you written down?

SELF: I have only written 'The Muslims are a Nation'.

JINNAH: And do you believe it?

SELF: I do.

JINNAH: (with a smile) What other questions have you got there?

SELF: The first is economic. Are the Muslims likely to be richer or poorer under Pakistan? And would you set up tariffs against the rest of India?

JINNAH: I'll ask you a question for a change. Supposing you were asked which you would prefer ... a rich England under Germany or a poor England free, what would your answer be?

SELF: It's hardly necessary to say.

JINNAH: Quite. Well, doesn't that make your question look a little shoddy? This great ideal rises far above mere questions of personal comfort or temporary convenience. The Muslims are a tough people, lean and hardy. If Pakistan means that they will have to be a little tougher, they will not complain. But why should it mean that? What conceivable reason is there to suppose that the gift of nationality is going to be an economic liability? A sovereign nation of a hundred million people – even if they are not immediately self-supporting and even if they are industrially backward – is hardly likely to be in a worse economic position than if its members are scattered and disorganized, under the dominance of two hundred and fifty million Hindus whose one idea is to exploit them. How can any European get up and say that Pakistan is 'economically impossible' after the Treaty of Versailles is really beyond my comprehension. The great brains who cut Europe into a ridiculous patchwork of conflicting and artificial boundaries are hardly the people to talk economics to us, particularly as our problem happens to be far simpler.

SELF: And does that also apply to defence?

JINNAH: Of course it applies to defence. Once again I will ask you a question. How is Afghanistan defended? Well? The answer is not very complicated. By the Afghans. Just that. We are a brave and united people who are prepared to work and, if necessary, fight. So, how does the question of defence present any peculiar difficulties? In what way do we differ from other nations? From Iran, for example? Obviously, there will have to be a transition period. We are not asking the British to quit India overnight. The British have helped to make this gigantic muddle, and they must stay and help to clear it up. But before they can do that, they will have to do a lot of hard thinking. And that reminds me – I have something I would like to show you.

'The British must realize,' he had said to me before we tackled the problem of Pakistan, 'that they have not a friend in the country. Not a friend.'

A Hindu politician would have said that at the top of his voice, with delight. Jinnah said it quietly, with regret. Here he was again. In his hand he carried a book.

JINNAH: You will remember I said, a moment ago, that the British would have to do a lot of hard thinking. It's a habit they don't find very congenial; they prefer to be comfortable, to wait and see, trusting that everything will come right in the end. However; when they do take the trouble to think, they think as dearly and creatively as any people in the world. And one of their best thinkers – at least on the Indian problem was old John Bright. Have you ever read any of his speeches?

SELF: Not since I left school.

JINNAH: Well, take a look at this. l found it by chance the other day.

He handed me the book It was a faded old volume, The Speeches of John Bright, and the date of the page at which it was opened was June 4th 1858. This is what the greatest orator in the IIouse of Commons said on that occasion:

How long does England propose to govern India? Nobody can answer that question. But be it 50 or 100 or 500 years, does any man with the smallest glimmering of common sense believe that so great a country, with its 20 different nationalities and its 20 different languages, can ever be bound up and consolidated into one compact and enduring empire confine? I believe such a thing to be utterly impossible.

I handed back the book.

JINNAH: What Bright said then is true to-day ... In fact, it's far more true – though, of course, the emphasis is not so much on the 20 nationalities as on the 2 ...the Muslim and the Hindu. And why is it more true? Why hasn't time brought us together? Because the Muslims are awake ...

because they've learnt, through bitter experience, the sort of treatment they may expect from the Hindus in a 'United India'. A 'United India' means a Hindu-dominated India. It means that and nothing else. Any other meaning you attempt to impose on it is mythical. 'India' is a British creation ... it is merely a single administrative' unit governed by a bureaucracy under the sanction of the sword. That is all. It is a paper creation, it has no basis in flesh, and blood.

SELF: The ironical thing is that your critics say that Pakistan itself is a British creation – that it is an example of our genius for applying the principle of 'divide and rule'.

JINNAH: (with some heat) The man who makes such a suggestion must have a very poor opinion of British intelligence, apart from his opinion of my own integrity. The one thing which keeps the British in India is the false idea of a United India, as preached by Gandhi. A United India, I repeat, is a British creation a myth, and a very dangerous myth, which will cause endless strife. As long as that strife exists, the British have an excuse for remaining. For once in a way, 'divide and rule' does not apply.

SELF: What you want is 'divide and quit?

JINNAH: You have put it very neatly.

SELF: You realize that all this will come as a something of a shock: to the British electorate?

JINNAH: Truth is often shocking. But why this truth in particular?

SELF: Because the average, decent. liberal-minded voter; who wishes Britain to fulfil her pledges, and grant independence to India, has heard nothing but the Congress point of view. The Muslims have hardly a single spokesman in the West.

JINNAH: (bitterly) I am well aware of that. The Hindus have organized a powerful Press and Congress Mahasabha are backed up by Hindu capitalists and industrialists with finance which we have not got.

SELF: As a result they believe that Congress is 'India,' and since Congress never tires of repeating that India is one and indivisble, they imagine that any attempt to divide it is illiberal, reactionary, and generally sinister. They seriously do believe this. I know that it is muddle-headed, but then a democracy such as ours, which has to make up its mind on an incredible number of complicated issues usually is muddle headed. What they have to learn is that the only liberal course, the only generous course, the only course compatible with a sincere intention to quit India and hand over the reins of government...

JINNAH: And the only safe course, you might add, is.

JINNAH: Pakistan!

VI

Jinnah Turns Apostle of Pakistan

Mohammad Ali Jinnah continued to work for Hindu Muslim unity and Mohandas Karamchand Gandhi made every gesture of cooperating with him in this cause. Nevertheless, Gandhi had transferred the arena of the Congress from the panelled chambers of lawyers to the streets of India. The masses and their agitation, *satyagraha* and civil disobedience, the breaking of law and order to register protest were contrary to the way Jinnah had grown up. Politically, his forte was argument, debate and crossing of swords but only on the floor of the legislature.

Jinnah could criticize British policy but would not condemn British rule. The question of India leaving the British Empire was not a part of his dictionary of objectives. He had his own code of ethics and he preferred to stick to them. For example, he considered the Khilafat movement ill-advised, if not also wrong. He did not support it, no matter how unpopular he made himself with the Muslims. The epitome of the classes was uncomfortable with the messiah of the masses. He was so irritated that he insisted on calling the Mahatma as Mr Gandhi.

Nevertheless, Jinnah could not help feeling more and more isolated. For example, in October 1920, Gandhi replaced Dr Annie Besant as the President of the Home Rule League. She had withdrawn because she felt that too much religion was being introduced into the League. Upon taking the chair, Gandhi changed the name of the institution to *Swaraj Sabha* in order to reach out to the non-English speaking people. Some object clauses were also changed such as complete *Swaraj* replaced self-government within the British Empire.

When an objection was raised to these changes, Gandhi declared that anyone who did not approve of the changes was free to resign. Jinnah along with nineteen other members decided to quit.

Jinnah's leadership however proved to be at the losing end. He took time to understand the damage his inflexibility was doing to him. He sounded contemptuous of Gandhi and told him that his approach would lead to disaster and that, in any case, he could not join, what the latter had described as new life in the Congress. Gandhi's mass appeal was for all to see and stalwarts like Motilal Nehru, Chittaranjan Das and others fell in line. Jinnah continued to be the odd fish floating out of the new water. He kept insisting that constitutional means were the only way to win freedom. When, in due course, he began realizing the import of the change, he had to restrain himself and he became more moderate, if not also polite.

In December 1920, the Congress session was held at Nagpur. A highlight of the session is best put in the words of Diwan Chaman Lall as quoted by Jinnah biographer Hector Bolitho:

> Diwan Chaman Lall has recalled the scene during the Congress meeting at Nagpur when Jinnah protested against Gandhi's extreme measures. Jinnah said, your way is the wrong way: mine is the right way – the constitutional way is the right way.

When Jinnah could not have his way, he decided to say goodbye to the Congress Party.

At the February 1921 session of the Muslim League in Calcutta, he referred to the Hindu messiah as Mahatma Gandhi. Nevertheless, his polite adjustment was more cosmetic than real. He, however, remained loyal to the cause of Hindu-Muslim unity because he was not in tune with Gandhi's approach of agitation. He had lost the sympathy of Hindu Congressmen. By sticking to his principles and joining the Hindus in opposing the appointment of the all white Simon Commission, he had also lost the sympathy of many Muslim members.

In 1924, Lord Birkenhead became the Secretary of State for India in the British government. He was surprised by the stubbornness of the various leaders who could not agree on fundamentals. He was impatient with the arguments leading to the boycott of the Simon Commission. All in all, Birkenhead was despondent. He believed that the Hindus and Muslims were irreconcilable and Bolitho has quoted him writing to Lord Reading that 'all the conferences in the world cannot bridge the unbridgeable'.

Nevertheless, in 1928, he challenged Indian leaders to produce a draft of a constitutional scheme of their desire. In response to the challenge, Motilal Nehru was nominated as the head of a committee appointed by an all party conference held in Bombay. When the draft was ready, it was found that the differences between the communities remained inexorable. The Muslims wanted a minimum of one-third reservations in the provinces as well as at the centre. Moreover, they insisted that the residuary powers should rest with the provinces.

Hindu thinking was just the opposite. It was prepared to accept reservations for Muslims but only in proportion to their population and not, necessarily, to the extent of one-third.

The Muslims were exasperated at the Congress rejecting the Muslim demands. Jinnah was also disheartened. According to his friends, he had tears in his eyes when he departed. He also declared that this was the final parting of ways. In the bargain, MA Jinnah stood isolated and alone. Dr Rafiq Zakaria, in his work, *The Man who Divided India*, Popular Prakashan, Mumbai, 2001, has summed up the situation in the statement:

> Disgusted with the state of affairs in India, Jinnah concluded that for the time being there was no place for him in Indian politics.

By the middle of 1928, Jinnah left for London where he bought for himself a house and began practising as a barrister.

Although he tried to keep away from politics, he could not help keeping in touch with what was happening in India. When the Round Table Conference was called to be held in January 1931 in London, Viceroy Irwin nominated Jinnah as one of the delegates from British India, as distinct from the princely states. Although at the conference, he continued to argue for ways and means to ensure Hindu Muslim unity, he felt disappointed to find that few others were sincere enough.

He was again invited to be a delegate to the Second Round Table Conference called later the same year. Although Jinnah attended the meet, he did not say much; if for no other reason, but for the fact that few of the participants were interested in listening to him. When he had sailed for England in 1928, he was disheartened because neither the Muslims nor Hindu members of the Congress and the League had much time for what he contended. Now, he was also ignored by the British who had assessed that Jinnah had little support of his people. He was not even invited to the Third Round Table Conference. He needed little more proof that even his British admirers had stopped caring for him.

Dr Rafiq Zakaria, in his book mentioned earlier, has regretted that:

> A frustrated and dejected Jinnah, disowned by the Muslims, distrusted by the Hindus, and discarded by the British, decided to reassert himself by changing his

> way. He threw away the baggage of the past. And with his own hands he dug the grave of Hindu-Muslim unity, to which he had devoted all his years in public life.

While writing *Jinnah* (John Murray, London, 1954), Hector Bolitho had interviewed Begum Liaquat Ali Khan and quoted her statement to him at considerable.

> We were married early in 1933 and we decided to go to Europe for our honeymoon. Liaquat and I arrived in London and we met Jinnah at a reception. Liaquat immediately began his appeal to Jinnah to return. I remember him saying 'They need someone who is un-purchaseable: lt was a word my husband liked. And it was true: Jinnah was un-purchaseable. He listened, but he did not answer at first: he talked of his life in England and of his contentment at Hampstead. But Liaquat was not to be denied. He said. 'You must come back. The people need you. You alone can put new life into the League and save it' Jinnah suddenly said, 'Well come to dinner on Friday.'
>
> "So we drove to Hampstead. It was a lovely evening. And his big house, with trees – apple trees – I seem to remember. And Miss Jinnah, attending to all his comforts. I felt that nothing could move him out of that security. After dinner, Liaquat repeated his plea, that the Muslims wanted Jinnah and needed him. I had hero-worshipped Mr Jinnah for a long time. I chirped in. 'And I'll make the women work for you, I'll bring them back into the fold.' He smiled at me and said, 'You are young, you do not know the women, you do not know the world.' But he listened to Liaquat, and in

> the end he said, 'You go back and survey the situation, test the feelings of all parts of the country. I trust your judgment. If you say, come back. I'll give up my life here and return.'"

Jinnah sailed for Bombay in January 1935 and began making friends with Muslim leaders and reorganising the Muslim League, He called the first session of the party in April 1936 wherein Sir Wazir Hasan was made the President and Sir Currimbhoy Ibrahim the Chairman of the reception committee. In his address, Sir Wazir made a brief reference to the two communities being two nations. Not long after the session, Jinnah became the permanent president of the League. He confided to his friend MC Chagla that he had lost all interest in Hindu-Muslim unity.

The Government of India Act of 1935 gave all Indian politicians an opportunity for activity and Jinnah made full use of it in spreading the network of his party. The response of the Muslim masses was also enthusiastic. Jinnah was successful in convincing them that the leadership of the Congress was responsible for suppressing the Muslims. Since it was a Hindu party, the Muslims could expect no good treatment from it. Whether it was the proposal to make Hindi the national language or of making *Vande Mataram* the national anthem, Jinnah seized every chance of inciting his Muslim followers against the Congress and Hindus. Jinnah had undergone a metamorphosis. From being the ambassador of Hindu Muslim unity, he tried to become a messiah who cried out that Islam was in danger. He abandoned his Saville Row suit, at least on public occasions, and donned the *sherwani* and *pyjama*. He could no longer avoid the masses and began to respond to Muslim crowds as he had seen Gandhi doing.

At the other end, he won over such reluctant separatists as Sir Sikander Hayat Khan and AK Fazlul Haq, then premiers of Punjab and Bengal provinces respectively. Poet Iqbal had also become his supporter. Many of his admirers as well as adversaries in Indian politics were astonished to find Jinnah so rabidly communal, but there he was leading the Muslims of India, unrivalled by any other leader. He had achieved politically in three years what he had not in the previous thirty. He now had a mass following.

He propounded the two nation theory and propagated it again and again and which was to build up towards the climax at Lahore on 23 March 1940 when the League passed the Pakistan Resolution. As President, he made an eloquent speech and an extract from it is quoted from the *Constitutional and Political History of Pakistan* (by Hamid Khan, Oxford University Press, Karachi, 2001):

> It has always been taken for granted mistakenly that the Mussalmans are a minority. The Mussalmans are a nation by any definition. What the military Government of India for 150 years has failed to achieve cannot be realized by the imposition of Central Federal Government except by means of armed force. The problem in India is not of an inter-communal character but manifestly of an international one and it must be treated as such.

> The Hindus and Muslims belong to two different civilizations which are based mainly on conflicting ideas and conceptions. To yoke together two such nations under a single state, one as a numerical minority and the other as a majority, must lead to growing discontent and final destruction of any fabric that may be so built up for the government of such a state.

Professor Hamid Khan's thesis is consistent with the Muslim League demand for a separate homeland and its leadership's insistence on a transfer on partition, of all Muslims to Pakistan.

VII

Get out of East Pakistan

The message from Noakhali in 1946 was: Hindus get out. Therc were widespread killings in the district. Gandhi promptly visited the area in order to stop the rioting. Nevertheless, he could not prevent the start of an exodus of Hindus leaving their homes and pouring into West Bengal.

It would be appropriate to quote here from *The Marginal Men*, a scholarly work by Prafulla K Chakrabarti, (Lumiere Books, Kalyani, 1990):

> *The second phase of the migration began with the pogrom of February 1950 in East Pakistan. This time the migrants came down like an avalanche. The entire administrative machinery cracked under the strain. The organised killing of the Hindus and looting of their property started at Bagerhat in East Pakistan and then it spread to other areas.*

The February riots started a chain reaction of organised violence in both Bengals and this time it was not a one-way traffic. For in 1950 not only Hindus came from the East to the West, terrified Muslims also started their trek from West Bengal to the other side of the border. But the refugees who sought shelter in government camps represented only a small fraction of the total influx. A large number of those who crossed into West Bengal, Tripura and Assam tried to fend, for themselves. The Census of 1951 shows the extent of the influx. In 1951 there were at least 3.5 million refugees in West Bengal.

When in the wake of the riots of 1950 a two-way movement of the migrants was in progress, the Nehru-Liaquat Ali Pact was concluded. The Pact provided for the restoration of the lands of the deserters of both countries in order to encourage them to return to their homes. It also provided for the enactment of laws by both countries for the implementation of its provisions. Accordingly, the Government of India promulgated an ordinance without delay and subsequently an Evacuee Properties Act, Act IX of 1951 – was passed, which provided:

A migrant Muslim family from West Bengal, returning within 31 March 1951 would be entitled to reoccupy the deserted property. It would be the duty of the District Magistrate to restore their property to them. If he was unable to do that, he would inform the authorities. If restoration of property was not possible, the Government would be responsible for their rehabilitation. If the owner of the deserted property failed to return, the property would be taken care of by the Supervising Committee which would have the right of leasing it for a one-year period.

The Act laid special stress on the protection of the right of the owner of the land. Moreover, he could also sell the land or exchange it. The provisions of the Act were implemented carefully. Nehru saw to it that they were implemented, although he did not consider it his business to see that a similar enactment was implemented in East Pakistan for the restoration of the properties of the evacuee Hindus. Nehru was so anxious that justice should be done to the evacuees that he sent AP Jain, the Rehabilitation Minister, to find out whether the West Bengal Government was dragging its feet in regard to the implementation of the Act. In 1952 the Fact Finding Committee, set up by the Central Rehabilitation Ministry, requested the West Bengal Rehabilitation Department to compile statistics relating to the amount of property restored to the Muslim evacuees under the provisions of the Act.

The Nehru-Liaquat Ali Pact was signed in April 1950 to put a stop to the massive two-way low of refugees in the wake of the riots of 1950. About 16 lakh Hindus migrated to India from East Pakistan and 2 lakh Muslims crossed into East Pakistan. The Pact provided for the return of the migrants to their homes and assured complete proprietary rights to the immovable properties they had left behind. Since the Nehru-Liaquai Ali Pact has not yet been formally abrogated, theoretically the East Pakistan refugees even today retain their titles to the immovable properties in East Pakistan. Thus the Pact kept before the East Pakistan refugees their illusory rights over properties left behind and deprived them of compensation while deluging the West Pakistan refugees with compensation for actual and supposed loss of immovable and movable properties in West Pakistan.

The story of Rehabilitation informs us that 'the concept

of compensation is the offspring of idealism and that the Prime Minister's compassionate concern for the millions dispossessed of their all by Partition found expression in the payment of compensation. Unfortunately this idealism and 'compassionate concern was limited to West Pakistan refugees. Nehru used the stillborn Pact of 1950 as an excuse to deny compensation to the East Pakistan refugees. Ajit Prasad Jain, the Central Rehabilitation Minister, was convinced that rehabilitation could not be complete without the payment of compensation. It would appear from the use of words like 'compassionate concern' for dispossessed millions or compensation being 'the offspring of idealism' that the Central Ministers suffered from amnesia regarding the East Pakistan refugees.

The pathos of the exodus from East Bengal, then called East Pakistan, which became Bangladesh in 1971, is best expressed in the words of Dr Triguna Sen in his Foreword to the quoted book. Dr Sen had been Vice Chancellor of Jadavpur University as well as Banaras Hindu University and was later also the Education Minister, Government of India.

It is extraordinary how passively West Bengal accepted after Partition the uprooting and the near-extermination of an entire people who participated almost to a man in the Indian struggle for freedom. True, the uprooting did not occur in East Pakistan in one swift swipe. It was a wasting disease. But it was this slow and surer process which ensured the steady expulsion of a completely denuded Hindu population through riots sponsored by an Islamic State and social, economic and religious persecution of the Hindus by Muslims in collusive partnership with the bureaucracy, which caused anger in West Bengal but did not provoke the Hindus to retaliatory reprisal. Only in 1950, in the wake of brutal massacres in different districts of East Bengal did the Hindus retaliate, and immediately a two-way exodus began which might have brought, about an unofficial transfer of population and a natural solution of the communal problem in West Bengal. But Nehru had reasons of his own to stop this natural solution of the problem and he bestirred himself immediately to stop this two-way movement by the Delhi Pact of 1950. The Pact stopped this two-way movement effectively and the Muslims who had left West Bengal returned and Nehru saw to it that their property was restored to them. But the exodus of the Hindus continued and lingers to this day. Even the Buddhist Chakmas oj the Chittagong Hill Tract are now being hounded out of the recesses of their hills.

The tragedy continues to unfold inexorably. On 27 May 2002, *The Statesman*, published from Kolkata and New Delhi, had the following to say in an editorial under the title of Sinister Design:

Another attempt on the life of a Buddhist monk in Chittagong in the wake of recent gruesome murders of two much respected religious heads – one a Buddhist and the other a Hindu – of the same area has made Bangladesh's minorities very insecure and badly tarnished the country's image. The suspicion has deepened as the police have refused to arrest the assailants when they are moving about freely with arms. What is worse is that the police have sought to explain the incidents in terms of sexual habits of the victims. Printed leaflets were distributed to this effect to coincide with the Home Minister's visit. The motive was also ascribed to possible occupation of vast properties

> *owned by the two ashrams. But this is not the truth. It is far more sinister as the religious leaders were the mainstay of the local Buddhist and Hindu communities which looked up to them for guidance and support. In fact, Gyanjyoti ran an orphanage for which he got liberal assistance from international Buddhist bodies. His murder outraged the Japanese government so much that its embassy in Dhaka while expressing shock sent a delegation to the ashram wanting the culprits to be punished. Interestingly Begum Zia's ministers called the two murders stray, isolated and unfortunate incidents.*

Actually the killings are a legacy of Zia-ur-Rahman and HM Ershad's policy of communalising Bangladesh politics by banishing secularism and making Islam the state religion. Large scale persecution of minorities by Begum Zia's armed cadres, following last October's 1946 parliamentary election, when at gun point they were told to go to India in their own interest, was also part of this legacy. Significantly, the two killings have coincided with the sinister public campaign that the Jamat-i-Islam has launched urging minorities to opt for an electorate as in the Pakistani days. The objective is to marginalise about 20 million people from Bangladesh's political mainstream.

In 1947 the percentage of the Hindu population was about 30 percent. In 1991 the proportion has come down to 10.3 percent as illustrated in Table I:

Ethnic cleansing has taken place elsewhere in the world. A comparison with what happened more recently in Cyprus, a part of Europe, is interesting.

Table I: Bangladesh
Percentage Distribution of Major Communities

Year	All Religions	Muslim	Hindu	Other
1961	100	80.4	18.5	1.1
1974	100	85.4	13.5	1.1
1981	100	86.6	12.1	1.2
1991	100	88.3	10.3	1.2

Source: Statistical Yearbook oj Bangladesh, 1980, 1990 & 1999: Census of population

The island country is situated about 40 miles south of Turkey and some 480 miles southeast of Greece. It was once inhabited by only 720,000 Greeks. During the high noon of the Ottoman expansion in 1571, it was invaded by the Turks, many of whom settled in the northern part of the island all of which was ruled from Istanbul. In 1878, the British took Cyprus on lease. The lease ended with the end of World War I and the island officially became a British colony in March 1925. It however ceased to be a part of the empire in 1960 when it was given independence. It then became the Republic of Cyprus. About 80 percent of the people were Greek speaking, while the balance was Turks.

Not uncommon to Muslims, the Turks found it difficult to coexist with the Christian Greeks. After the displacement of the Ottoman rule in 1878, Cyprus ceased to be a Dar ul Islam since the writ of the *sharia* ceased to run. But it became a land of dispute or warfare or a *Dar ul Harb* to the Turkish settlers. However unwelcome the change of rulers, they had to tolerate it due to the sheer might of imperial Britain. The situation changed as soon as the British left. Yet, the *Dar ul Harb* status could not be changed because the Turkish population was only about one/fifth of the total. The corollary of this hopelessness was separatism which however could not be spontaneously implemented by the Turkish speaking minority.

The Muslims therefore invited the Republic of Turkey to invade Cyprus in 1974. Obviously, the government of the island was too small to resist the invasion. Turkey imposed partition of the country in 1975. The people of the separated portion made an unilateral declaration of independence in 1983 and adopted the name Turkish Republic of Northern Cyprus. Its independence was recognized by Istanbul only.

It is noteworthy that the Muslim Turks and the Christian Greeks lived across Cyprus in varying numbers. The northern part had many Greek speaking people. Remember, until the 16th century, the island was inhabited only by them; the Turks came in from 1571 onwards. What was particularly tragic was that in the wake of the invasion in July and August 1974, the Turkish invaders from the mainland carried out ruthless ethnic cleansing. As many as 200,000 Greek Cypriots were expelled from the northern area by force. They had to leave their homes and properties behind and move to the Greek majority areas in the South. They became refugees in their own country. All this happened well before partition was imposed in 1975, not to speak of the unilateral declaration of independence in 1983.

After the ethnic cleansing of 1974, some 12,000 Greek Cypriots, mostly older people, insisted on staying put in the northern area. Over the following 20 years the figure was down to 715 and is probably nil by now. The experience of Cyprus is reminiscent of what has happened not only in the western wing of Pakistan and also Bangladesh. Similar ethnic cleansing continues inexorably in Bangladesh. Rather than repeating the well known tragic tale of Bangladeshi Hindus, the story is portrayed in the following two tables:

Table II: Bangladesh
Census of Population by Religion in Numbers

Year	All Religions	Muslim	Hindu	Others
1974	7,14.78.000	6,10.39.000	96,73.000	7.66,000
1981	8,71,20.00	7.54,87,000	1.05,70,000	10,63,000
1991	1,06,34,992	9,38.81,029	1,11,78,866	12,55.097

Source: Statistical Yearbook of Bangladesh. 1990, 1999: Census of Population

Table III
Percentage Distribution & Variation of Major Communities by Religion

Year	All	Muslim	Hindu	Others	Communities %	Variation %	Variation %
1901	100	66.1	—	33	—	0.9	—
1911	100	67.2	10.9	31.5	4.3	1.3	49.1
1921	100	68.1	6.8	30.6	2.2	1.3	10.2
1931	100	69.5	9.2	29.4	2.8	1.1	5.0
1941	100	70.3	9.3	28.0	12.4	1.7	76.9
1951	100	76.3	9.2	22.0	21.4	1.1	37.3
1961	100	80.4	26.9	18.5	1.5	1.1	22.2
1974	100	85.4	49.3	13.5	3.1	1.1	34.4
1981	100	86.6	23.7	12.1	9.3	1.2	38.8
1991	100	88.3	24.4	10.5	5.8	1.2	18.1

Source: Statistical Yearbook of Bangladesh 1999: Census of Population, 1991

VIII

Population Transfer Between Greece and Turkey*

The history of population transfer in Europe dates back to 22 September 1609 AD when, by a Spanish royal order, 300,000 Moriscos were expelled. A Morisco or a little Moor was a Spaniard of European descent who had been converted to Islam seven centuries earlier and who refused to return to the Christian fold. Many of them were suspected of religious perfidy and political infidelity for over a century. They were resettled in Algeria, Morocco and Tunisia.

The next milestone in the history of population transfer was when on 18 October 1685, Louis XIV, the Grand

---

* This chapter is based on a book by Stephen P Ladas called *The Exchange of Minorities, Bulgaria, Greece and Turkey*, The Macmillan Company, New York, 1932.

Monarch of France revoked the Edict of Nantes. More than nine decades earlier, by this edict, King Henry IV had granted to the Protestants of the country, called Huguenots, the right to worship freely. As a result of the revocation, within the following few years some 400,000 Huguenots emigrated to England, Prussia, Holland and America.

This is so much for what we in India would call medieval history. Soon after World War I ended, in 1919 Bulgaria and Greece signed at Neuilly a convention for the reciprocal migration of ethnics living in each other's country.

This exchange of peoples was followed in 1923 with a Turko-Greek convention for the compulsory exchange of their respective ethnics. This convention was a result of the declaration by Turkey that it would refuse to allow the repatriation of over a million Greeks who were driven from or had left Turkey since 1912. Thus the convention chiefly served to register and confirm an accomplished fact, although it also permitted Greece to compel its Muslim population to migrate to Turkey.

The seeds of the Turko-Greek conflict were sown with the Muslim conquest of Constantinople and the empire surrounding it way back in 1453. Over the centuries conversions took place and Greece and other areas in the vicinity had to suffer oppression by the Ottoman rulers. During World War I, the rulers intensified the work of Ottoman-ising the empire and its people. The intention was to make Turkey a homogeneous state by either assimilating, or by eradicating people or by expelling the minorities. Many Christian Greeks fled to Greece.

In the fall of 1922, the Greco-Turkish War, a sequel of World War I, was caused by the occupation of Smyrna and Western Asia Minor by Greece at the behest of the *Allies* and came to an abrupt end with the decisive victory of the Turks and the precipitate retreat of the Greek army.

As a result, almost a million people were *thrown on the borders* of Greece in the space of a few months. Following the Convention of Lausanne of 1923, the remaining Greeks in Turkey, excluding Constantinople or Istanbul, where the Eastern Church is headquartered, left the country under the auspices of the Mixed Commission. The total was over 150,000 persons. Under the same convention, the Muslims of Greece, with the exception of those residing in Western Thrace, were compelled to leave for Turkey. They numbered about 400,000.

The Turkish government was well aware that the Greek government would never, of its own will, consent to receiving the Greeks in exchange for the Muslims living in Greece. It decided, accordingly, to force the hand of the Greek government by expelling the Greeks from the Aegean coast regions or deporting them into the interior of Anatolia with the intent of harassing them. The systematic implementation of this plan began in early 1914. Within a few months 150,000 Greeks were forced to leave the western coast of Asia Minor to seek refuge in Greece. Another 50,000 were deported to the interior of Anatolia.

Mr Venizelos, representing Greece, responded to the Turkish Minister, accepting the proposal of an exchange of population, provided the free and spontaneous character of the migration was secured and the properties of the migrants were appraised and disposed off. He also proposed that the exchange be extended to Thrace. The Greco-Turkish Agreement of 1914 may be deemed to be the forerunner of the Convention of Neuilly of 1919 and the Convention of Lausanne of 1923.

The convention of 30 January 1923 regarding the exchange of Greek and Turkish population, was a part of the peace settlement with Turkey. It was proposed that the exchange should be carried out within three months. Lord Curzon, the British Foreign Secretary, expressed his preference for a compulsory exchange, as only in this way could the expected results be obtained. On a voluntary basis the exchange would take months, *whereas what was wanted was first, to get the Turkish population into Eastern Thrace ... and, second, to provide for the accommodation in Greece of the refugees.* He also proposed to exempt the Greeks of Constantinople from the exchange in the interests of Turkey and to set against these people the Turkish population of Western Thrace.

> Lord Curzon said that he deeply regretted that the solution should be the compulsory exchange of population, a thoroughly bad and vicious solution, for which the world would pay a heavy penalty for a hundred years to come. He detested having anything to do with it. But to say it was a suggestion of the Greek government was ridiculous. It was a solution enforced by the action of the Turkish government in expelling these people from Turkish territory. In reply to this,

> Ismet Pasha of Turkey remarked that Lord Curzon had said that he detested the compulsory exchange of populations; but at the meeting of the Commission on the 1st December, Lord Curzon had declared that no solution was possible except the exchange of populations, and that, as voluntary exchange could not give any result, recourse must be had to compulsory exchange.

The convention and the protocol were signed at Lausanne on 30 January, 1923. The convention was to come into force, in accordance with its 19 articles immediately after the ratification of the Treaty of Peace by Greece and Turkey.

The Treaty of Peace between the British Empire, France, Italy, Japan, Greece, Rumania, the Serb-Croat-Slovene state, and Turkey, signed at Lausanne on 24 July 1923, was ratified by Turkey on 23 August 1923, and by Greece on 25 August 1923.

The convention concerning the exchange of Greek and Turkish populations consisted of 19 articles. Article 1 laid down the principle of compulsory exchange by providing as follows:

> As from 1st May, 1923, there shall take place a compulsory exchange of Turkish nationals of the Greek Orthodox religion established in Turkish territory, and of Greek nationals of the Moslem religion established in Greek territory. These persons shall not return to live in Turkey or Greece respectively without the authorization of the Turkish Government or of the Greek Government respectively.

Article 2 defined the persons who were not to be included

in the exchange. These were the Muslims of Western Thrace and Christian Greeks of Constantinople. Article 3 stipulated that the Muslims and Greeks who had left the Greek and Turkish territories respectively since 18 October, 1912, were to be considered as included in the exchange. The first instalment of Greeks sent to Greece were all to be able bodied men belonging to the Greek population detained in Turkey and whose families had already left Turkish territory. In this respect the protocol annexed to the Convention provided that, by way of exception to Article 1 of the convention, such able bodied Greeks were to be released by the Turkish government on the signing of the Treaty of Peace and the facilities for their departure were to be provided at the same time. It was further stipulated, in Article 16, that no pressure would be exercised on the other people to leave before the date fixed for their departure by the Mixed Commission. Also, persons exempted from the exchange were free to exercise their right to remain or return to the excepted districts.

No obstacle was to be placed in the way of the departure of a person belonging to the populations which were to be exchanged. Convicts and persons to be tried for crimes were to be handed over to the authorities of the country whither they were going. Persons who had already departed were to acquire the nationality of the country of destination on the date of signing of the convention. Persons, who left in the future, would lose the nationality they had and acquire the nationality of the country of destination on their arrival in the territory of the latter country (Articles 6 and 7).

The exchange would not prejudice the rights of property and monetary assets of the exchanged people. They were to be free to take away or arrange for the transport of their movable property. They could also leave behind property, in which case the local authorities were to draw up an inventory and valuation of such property. Immovable and movable property of the exchanged populations was to be sold off by the Mixed Commission. This included property of persons who had departed since 18 October 1912, independently of any measures taken with respect to such property, such as confiscation, forced sale etc. Expropriated property was to be appraised afresh by the Mixed Commission. Damages to, or revenues from such properties of refugees were to be appraised by the Mixed Commission (Articles 5, 8, 9 and 10).

The Mixed Commission was to consist of four members representing Greece, four representing Turkey, and three chosen by the League of Nations from among nations of countries which did not take part in World War I. The commission was constituted on 17 September 1923, less than a month after the coming into force of the convention, and met for the first time at Athens on 8 October 1923. The commission to supervise and facilitate the execution of the convention was to be set up within a month from the coming into force of the convention. Its constitution, duties and powers were determined by Articles 11, 12 and 13.

The sums due to the exchanged population of each country on account of property liquidated by the Mixed Commission was to constitute a government debt from the country where the liquidation took place, to the government of the country to which the proprietors emigrated. The exchanged populations were entitled, in principle, to receive in their new country property of a value equal to and of the same nature, as that which they had left behind. Provisions were made for settlement of accounts between the two governments as a result of the liquidation (Article 14).

Besides the convention concerning the exchange of Greek and Turkish populations, two other agreements were signed at the close of the conference at Lausanne. They were meant to extend the benefits of the convention to Muslims who had left Greece prior to 1912, and imposed on the Greek government the obligation to buy the properties of such persons situated in the old provinces of Greece.

The Declaration as to Muslim properties in Greece, signed at Lausanne on 24 July 1923 stipulated that the property rights of Muslims who were not included in the provisions of the convention concerning the exchange of populations, and who had left Greece, including the island of Crete, before 18 October 1912, or who had always resided outside Greece, should not be prejudiced. These persons were to have the right to freely dispose off their properties.

The Muslims might ask the good offices of the Mixed Commission for the sale of their properties. This would not however involve any obligation on the Greek state to buy such properties. The Declaration was made on condition of reciprocity in favour of Greek proprietors who had left Turkey before 18 October 1912, or who had always resided outside Turkey.

The only criterion of the exchangeability of a person, besides the fact that he was a national of the country which he was compelled to leave, was that of religion. The result would be that the Albanian Muslims resident in Greece and Armenians, Syrians, Russians, Rumanians, etc., of the Greek Orthodox religion in Turkey would be compelled to emigrate. This consequence would be avoided if the criterion of religion was understood in a broader sense by the Turkish rulers. Indeed, it was not meant to be taken strictly as an equivalent to faith or creed, but as a compound of ethnological, political and religious elements. Religion was a safe criterion, less as a demarcation between the followers of two different faiths, than as a sharp dividing line between the two ethnic peoples and, to a certain extent, political entities.

The Greek Orthodox religion was an ethnic entity within the Turkish Empire, having as its head the Greek Ecumenical Patriarch of Constantinople. He was recognized by official acts of the Empire as the head of the Greek Church as well as of the Greek nation, and he was given not only religious but also administrative and judicial powers within that nation. When Greece became an independent state in 1830, its people maintained a spiritual connection with the Greek Ecumenical Patriarch and that part of the Greek nation remaining under Turkish rule. Thus, the Greek Orthodox religion was in a sense the external link of union between the two parts of the Greek nation, the free and the unredeemed. As such, it was considered the best criterion for defining Greek national minorities in Turkey.

It is uncanny how comparable the situation in Greece and Turkey was in 1923 with the conditions prevailing in the Indian subcontinent in 1947. The pains taken by the League of Nations to the last detail in order to facilitate the exchange of population are remarkable.

Demand for Pakistan

THE DEMAND for the new state was led by men who resided in the provinces of Bihar, Bombay and United Provinces (UP). MA Jinnah was a Gujarati whereas Nawabzada Liaquat Ali Khan hailed from what is now Haryana. To accommodate the expected *mohajirs*, the Muslim League governments encouraged ethnic cleansing whereby non-Muslims were forced to move to Hindustan. The cleansing was thorough in the western wing of Pakistan and less thorough in East Pakistan.

However, not many Muslims migrated or undertook *hijrat*. Punjab was the only province where there was an exchange of population. For the rest, whether Baluchistan, North West Frontier Province, Sindh or Bengal, the exodus was largely one way into India by the Hindus. There was no exchange. Overwhelmingly, the Muslims resident in the rest of Hindustan stayed put. Some who had migrated even came back. The assurances by Hindu leaders made all the difference. The Constitution of India was also attractive for Muslims. Articles 29 and 30 offered several special privileges to them. As a result, Jinnah's dream remained unfulfilled, which explains why the agenda of Partition is still unfinished.

On the other hand, Hindustan's single biggest obsession since Independence has been its minority which is an euphemism for Muslims. A separate civil code, based on the *sharia*, continues to be followed for them even as it is in violation of Article 44, a directive principle of policy in the Constitution.

The ugliest symptom of minority obsession is the frequency of communal riots, which is again an euphemism for Hindu-Muslim riots. Or else, occasionally there should be a Hindu Christian riot, at least in Kerala and Tamil Nadu, where Christians are in greater numbers than Muslims. Yet there has only been Muslims rioting whether in Coimbatore or in Kochi.

Why? The author when he tried to find out, found the clue in the provocations of the Muslim League leaders. The Muslim League showed that it meant business, first by Direct Action begun with the Great Calcutta Killings of August 1946 and then with the riots during Partition and the subsequent ethnic cleansing.

In the absence of a *Dar-ul-Islam* or a land where the writ of the *sharia* runs, many Muslims feel they cannot fulfil themselves as *momins* or faithfuls.

In response to the 23 March 1940 resolution of the Muslim League for the creation of Pakistan, a number of questions were raised. One of the most important was: no matter where the line of demarcation was drawn, there would be Hindus, Muslims and Sikhs on either side in a minority. They would overnight become aliens and foreigners in their own homes. Mohammed Ali Jinnah initially evaded this question, but later began to promise protection to the minorities. However, there was no question of Hindus and Sikhs obtaining citizenship or equal status with the nationals of Pakistan. If they could, why divide India was his question? Not being satisfied himself with his own logic, he suggested an exchange of population as the realistic solution.

As if to avoid exploding a bomb or to shock people, Jinnah was slow and gentle in bringing up the question of population transfer. But as wise and educated as he was, it is fair to believe that he was familiar with the European experience where, at the beginning of the 20th century, some two and a half million people had undertaken transfer of residence across national frontiers. Muslim Bulgarians were resettled in Turkey and many Turks were transferred to Bulgaria in pursuance of the Turko-Bulgarian Convention of 1913. This was also done officially under the Treaty of Lausanne signed on 30 January 1923 between Turkey and Greece.

Professor M Mujeeb, Vice-Chancellor of Jamia Millia Islamia, New Delhi had an interesting experience. In his words, quoted from his book *Islamic Influence on Indian Society*, Meenakshi Prakashan, Meerut, 1972:

> At a party given during the UN General Assembly Session in 1949 I had the pleasure of being placed next to the Turkish representative. He looked at my name card, saw that I was a Muslim and at once asked, are there still any Muslims in India? The impression then created does not yet seem to have been removed and it is believed that the sub-continent had been divided between Muslims and Hindus, with all Muslims on the one side and all Hindus on the other.

Jinnah must surely have been aware of the philosophical mainspring of Pakistan. Ever since British captured power and the consequent displacement of Muslim rule, there was widespread feeling that a *Dar-ul-Islam* in India had been replaced by a *Dar-ul-Harb* or a land of struggle. There is a principle as old as Islam that a *jihad* has to be fought for acquiring a *Dar-ul-Islam*. On the other hand, when there is no hope of achieving it, a *Dar-ul-Harb* cannot be tolerated indefinitely. The solution for the Muslims then was *hijrat* or migration to a land of Islam. Incidentally, devout faithful believe that they were fighting *jihad* against the British right through the 19th century. A *hijrat* was also undertaken by several hundred thousand Muslims who migrated to Afghanistan in 1920 on their realisation that the British would not allow the Sultan to continue on the throne of Turkey and thus remaining the *khalifa* for all Sunnis. Nearly 20,000 Indian Muslims succeeded in entering and settling in Afghanistan.

For the Muslim leaders therefore the idea of a population transfer was neither novel nor surprising. Even Prophet

Muhammad had undertaken *hijrat* from Mecca to Medina while founding Islam. No wonder then that Khan Iftikhar Hussain of Mamdot had said that the exchange of population offered a very practical solution for the problem of the Muslims, reported by *Dawn*, 3 December 1946. Pir Ilahi Bux, the Sindhi leader, had said that he welcomed an exchange of population for the safety of the minorities, as it would put an end to all communal disturbances as reported by *Dawn*, on 4 December 1946. So also felt Raja Ghazanfar Ali who later became Pakistan's envoy to New Delhi. *Dawn*, of 19 December 1946, reported his having asked for the alteration of the population map of India. His detailed plea is reproduced in a clipping given in this chapter. Sir Ivan Jenkins, the Governor of Punjab, had then observed that by asking for an exchange of population, the Muslim League was planning to forcibly drive away Hindus from Punjab.

It was implicit in these statements that the League's objective was to undertake ethnic cleansing soon after Partition. That this was not mere conjecture was proved by the fact that almost all Hindus were driven out from West Pakistan in a matter of two to three years. Evidently, the League leadership had fears that ethnic cleansing on their side would invite a similar action in Hindustan, causing untold miseries to their Muslim brethren. In any case, the *Dar-ul-Islam* that they were pursuing was for all Muslims of the subcontinent. Why should those, who happened to be in Hindustan, be condemned to live indefinitely in a hopeless *Dar-ul-Harb?*

These were no stray threats either by Mamdot or the Pir Jinnah, while addressing a press conference at Karachi on 25 November 1946, said that the authorities, both central and provincial, should immediately take up the question of exchange of population, as reported by *Dawn*, on 26 November, 1946. Sir Feroze Khan Noon, who later rose to be Prime Minister, had earlier on 8 April 1946, threatened to re-enact the murderous orgies of Chengez Khan and Halaqu Khan if non-Muslims took up an obstructive attitude against population exchange. Ismail Chundrigar, who also eventually rose to be Prime Minister of Pakistan, had said that the British had no right to hand over Muslims to a subject people over whom they had ruled for 500 years. Mohammad Ismail, a leader from Madras had declared that the Muslims of India were in the midst of a *jihad*. Shaukat Hayat Khan, son of the former Premier of Punjab, Sir Sikander Hayat Khan, had threatened, while the British were still in India, of a rehearsal of what the Muslims would do to the Hindus eventually. The point that came through clearly was that transfer of population was an integral part of the demand for Pakistan.

What the politicians said was confirmed by Professor M Mujeeb, in his erudite work. He said that the Muslim League demanded the creation of a separate homeland for Indian Muslims. He further stated that in the elections held early in 1946, the League, whose dominant manifesto was the creation of Pakistan, secured 425 seats out of 492 reserved for Muslims. The League insisted that the right to a separate homeland should be conceded first and all other negotiations could be held thereafter. He went on to say:

> The decision in regard to exchange of populations applied only to Eastern and Western Punjab. A large proportion of the Hindus in the North West Frontier Province and in Sind would have stayed on if they could. On the other hand, there would have been much less of immigration of the Hindus of East Pakistan into West Bengal and anti-Muslim sentiment in eastern and northern India would not have been constantly revived.

These thoughts were no doubt unsavoury, if not also repulsive to thc Hindu, but it has to be admitted that the Muslim League leaders had a clear vision. Their demand for not only partition but also population transfer might have seemed abhorrent, but the fact was that the Muslim leadership had thought through the implications of creating Pakistan. If a division was to be made, it had to be thorough and comprehensive. It is the Congress leadership which faltered in thought and floundered in action. It would have seen a different matter, if they had not conceded Partition. But having agreed to the division, quite clearly on the basis of the two nation theory propounded by the League, did they have the right of being confused over its consequences? If they could not visualize what was to follow, they had every opportunity to consult the Hindu leaders of East Bengal and Hindu and Sikh leaders of Punjab, Sind and North West Frontier Province. But those who were likely to be affected the most were ignored. This made the blundering by the Congress leaders quite unforgivable.

Uncannily, once MA Jinnah took over leadership of the Muslims, the initiative was held by the League with the Congress being continually on the defensive. Nevertheless, the Congress did not even react. However ill-conceived Partition might have seemed to many a Hindu, as well as to a number of Muslim leaders, like Maulana Abul Kalam Azad and Khan Abdul Ghaffar Khan, the fact was that Jinnah achieved it on his own terms.

The League's demand for an exchange of population was loudly voiced and widely debated. Merely to get a flavour of the contemporary reports, read a few clippings from the 1946 issues of Dawn. It was a daily then published from Delhi, and now from Karachi. The journal was founded by Jinnah.

The Muslim League demanded an exchange of population especially through 1946. Simultaneously, it carried on Direct Action, following the Great Calcutta Killing of August 1946, especially in the Punjab, were the party felt ethnic cleansing was most necessary. Come 1947, the rioting escalated in order to make sure that the Hindus, including Sikhs, emigrated. The carnage continued after Independence; by 1948, the western wing of Pakistan had been cleansed of Hindus and Sikhs. The eastern wing, or what is now Bangladesh, was emulating the western wing although at a more gradual pace.

In sharp contrast, the Congress leaders, whether in government or outside, ignored the League's demand for an exchange of population. Mahatma Gandhi was busy singing *ishwar allah tero nam* and repeating that Ram and Rahim were one. Although Jawaharlal Nehru called himself a British prime minister of India, he was actually playing the role of a Muslim although he happened to be a Hindu. He had come to be known as a Fabian or non-revolutionary socialist. A socialist had to be spontaneously secular. Vallabhbhai Patel was about the only top Congressman who warned Muslims that those who did not migrate to Pakistan had to be loyal to Hindustan.

How far Nehru was impartial between religions and whether he was biased is best verified by what is codified in the Constitution of India whose passing he led and directed as Prime Minister.

These articles were based on what was drafted well before Partition had been decided. Speaking in the Constituent Assembly on 8 December, 1948, Jawaharlal Nehru said:

> Mr Vice President, Sir, we are on the last lap of our long journey. Nearly two years ago, we met in this hall and on that solemn occasion it was my high privilege to move a Resolution which has come to be known as the Objective Resolution. This is rather a prosaic description of that Resolution because it embodied something more than mere objectives, although objectives are big things in the life of a nation. It tried to embody, insofar as it is possible in cold print, the spirit that lay behind the Indian people at the time. It is difficult to maintain the spirit of a nation or a people at a high level all the time and I do not know if we have succeeded in doing that. Nevertheless, I hope that it is in that spirit that we shall consider it in detail, always using that Objective Resolution as the yard measure with which to test every clause and phrase in this Constitution.

The Objective Resolution was introduced in the same Constituent Assembly by Jawaharlal Nehru on 13 December, 1946 well before the decision had been taken by the British government, the Communist Party, the Muslim League and others, to partition the country.

Even the declaration by the British Prime Minister, Clement Attlee that India would be granted independence: was not made until 20 February, 1947. The decision to partition the country had to wait till 3 June, 1947.

There were eight clauses in the Objective Resolution of which No.6 read: wherein adequate safeguards shall be provided for minorities, backward and tribal areas, and depressed and other backward classes. These quotations are from the Constituent Assembly Debates, Books 1 and 2, published by the Lok Sabha Secretariat, New Delhi, and reprinted in 1999.

Evidently, the privileges contemplated for the minorities were an endeavour to avoid partition by dissuading the Muslims, especially the League, from insisting on division of the country. Nevertheless, the League successfully insisted on the implementation of the two nation theory, whereby it was Pakistan for the Muslims and Hindustan for the rest. Even though it may be difficult to accept that in this context even for the Muslims, Jinnah was more reasonable than Nehru. The proof of this contention is the agreement that Jinnah signed with Raja Maheshwar Dayal Seth, General Secretary of the All India Hindu Mahasabha, several years before Partition. The essence of the agreement was that in the event of Partition,

Muslims would not expect any safeguards in Hindustan.

Although secularism to this day remains the signature tune of the Congress party, yet faith in its ideals has never taken root. In fact, what precisely secularism means in India has never been clarified. The 16th century European definition was separation of the Church from the State; non-interference of the clergy in affairs of government. The Marxist concept was to abolish religion from the life of the people, whereas tolerance has been a hallmark of the Hindu ethos since the beginning. Therefore, the question of introducing secularism into the affairs of India appears to have been unnecessary. The way secularism has been practiced in India, the spirit of tolerance has been distorted. Hindu - Muslim riots are a symptom of this distortion.

It is noteworthy that of the constitutions of 391 countries that the author has seen, only four mention the word secular. They are the Albanian, French, Indian and Namibian constitutions. Incidentally, when our Constitution was adopted in 1950, there was no mention of secularism. The term was brought in by Indira Gandhi during the Emergency in 1976.

Many an opposition member was then in jail. Nevertheless, if the Indian State had remained impartial towards all the religions, the distortion of tolerance might not have been so widespread. Unfortunately, government policies have shown a distinct bias towards the Muslims. For example, the Hajj subsidy: no comparable concession is provided to members of any other faith. If a Roman Catholic proposes to go to the Vatican, he has to pay the full fare for his trip. So would a Jew if he were to go to Jerusalem. The Hindu does not get anything for going on a pilgrimage.

One of the Directive Principles of State Policy contained in Article 44 of the Constitution requires the introduction of a Common Civil Code; one law common to all citizens. Seventy years have passed since the Constitution was adopted, yet there is no sign of the country having one personal law. If the Muslims were to insist on their own distinctive personal law, why should the State not also demand of them to accept the *sharia* with regard to criminal law. Minority educational institutions are allowed to be run freely although they are subsidised by the state, whereas, Hindu institutions are denied any subsidy. So discriminatory is this law that the much respected Rama Krishna Mission was driven to claim that it is a minority organisation!

Why was the Minorities Commission established? Are not minorities human? Their interests could have been looked after by the National Human Rights Commission. Evidently, there was systematic intention by the Government of India at some point in time to keep alight the flame of minority-ism. If they got integrated into the national mainstream, they might cease to be useful vote banks!

It is unlikely that the Muslim community or its leadership initially demanded any of these favours from the Indian state. Who would understand Muslim aspirations better than Qaid-e-Azam Jinnah, especially in the years around Independence and Partition? It is not widely known that Jinnah entered into a written agreement, several years before Partition, with the All India Hindu Mahasabha the General Secretary of which at the time was Raja Maheshwar Dayal Seth. According to the agreement, the country was to be partitioned soon after Independence with the help of a plebiscite. There was to be no corridor between the Muslim areas of the northwest and the northeast of India although they could form a single sovereign state. Government machinery was to be provided for facilitating the transfer of population. Above all, it said:

> In the event of separation the Muslims shall not demand any safeguard for the Muslim minority in Hindustan. It will be open to the two Indias to arrange on a reciprocal basis safeguards for religious minorities in the respective states. (Page 301, *Indian Muslim: A Political History by Ram Gopal*, Asia Publishing House, New York, 1959).

It is well known how the minorities were dealt with subsequently by Pakistan. Dr Rafiq Zakaria, in his recent book *The Man Who Divided India*, Popular Prakashan, Mumbai, 2001, has described what happened in that country. Some Indian Muslims living in India asked Mr Jinnah on the eve of partition:

> What is to happen to us who are being left behind? He assured them that if any harm came to them, Pakistan would retaliate against the Hindus under its control. But he could not have been serious about that for he must have known that after the hate campaign he had unleashed against the Hindus, few of them would have dared to stay on in his Pakistan and they did not; they

> fled in the most excruciating circumstances – many died on the way, the rest reached India with nothing.

Although the expression 'ethnic cleansing' was not used, what happened in the western wing of Pakistan was just that. In the eastern wing, something similar has been happening but in a chronic, rather than an acute manner.

In fairness to the Muslim League and the community it represented, it was forthright about its non-secular intentions ever since it was founded in 1906. One of its essential rules was that only a Muslim could become a member of the party. The League's demand for separate electorates was conceded by the Lucknow Pact which was signed between the Congress and the Muslim League in 1916. While writing in his journal *Al Hilal* during 1913, Maulana Abul Kalam Azad had said that no Muslim need join any political party. Islam itself is a party whose name is Hizbullah. The Imam and the Sultan are rolled into one and this integrated concept was personified by the Caliph or the representative of the Holy Prophet. But for the Congress Party to concede separate electorates for the two communities was to bury its secular credentials.

Whatever hope might have persisted for the practice of secularism in India, was finally dashed to the ground when the Congress conceded the League's demand for Partition. Pakistan for Muslims and Hindustan for the rest was the understanding of the League.

No matter what the ideals of the Congress leaders might have been, to agree to Partition was to endorse the two nation theory. The Muslims of undivided India, it was contended by the League, were a nation separate from the rest of Indians. They, therefore, needed a separate homeland. Pakistan was not merely a piece of territory vivisected from the rest of India. It was also a home for all the Muslims to gather in, to live in and flourish. The Congress Party let the country's territory be divided, but did not follow through with the transfer of people. Instead, its government enshrined discriminatory temptations-Articles 29 and 30, in the Constitution to induce Muslims to stay back.

The failure of Hindustan to fall in line with Islamic separatism was unfortunate, if not also unwarranted. New Delhi appointed as its first High Commissioner to Pakistan a gentleman called Sri Prakasa who proved to be a quisling or *gaddaar*. Read in his own words as printed in his book called Pakistan: *Birth and Early Days*, published by Meenakshi Prakashan, Delhi, 1965.

> Our Government did its very best to make it possible for Muslims to come back to India. Naturally they could not take everyone. The problem of sheer accommodation was exceedingly difficult. We had to find room for many millions of Punjabi and Sindhi Hindus, and we could not possibly have all the Muslims also with us, even though we had no animosity for them, and we really desired that they should stay with us.
>
> I had to face three exoduses. I have already spoken of the employees of the Central Government and then of Sindhi Hindus. The third was of Indian Muslims who had come to Pakistan in a fit of great enthusiasm for a new homeland that they had obtained, and where they

> have hoped that prosperity would be waiting with open arms to welcome them.
>
> To the Banaras weavers, I said: "Why have you come here? No one wants you here. Do get back home. Why do you want to destroy my city? It is you who have made it famous in the world." I immediately used to issue permits to them to go back. This caused some misunderstanding between me and my assistants in my office. They looked at the situation with different eyes. The Government of India also later changed its policy in this behalf. Formerly they encouraged Indian Muslims to remain where they were. Later, when they saw that not a single Hindu was allowed to remain in Pakistan, and that all of them were coming away, they felt it was necessary that at least as many Muslims should go away as was the number of Hindus who had come. There was obviously not sufficient room for everyone in India as she now became.
>
> Constitutionally speaking, I was more responsible for them because they were Indians, than for the Hindus in Pakistan because these were the primary charge of the government there. The situation being what it was at that time, the position was reversed; and the Indian High Commission came to be in a way in charge of the welfare of the Hindus in Pakistan while the Government of Pakistan was supposed to have the duty of looking after migrating Indian Muslims.

In their heart of hearts Hindus have grown up to hate Muslims. At the same time, by and large Muslims do not hate but certainly harbour contempt for the Hindus. This mutually antagonistic attitude has reflected the Hindu-Muslim equation right through the centuries, till the British began to assume power in India. Until then, the Muslim was the ruler and the Hindu, the subject across large tracts of the country. No doubt, there was a phase when the Marathas gained influence in many parts of India, but their domination was neither permanent nor widespread enough to correct the Hindu-Muslim imbalance that had grown over the centuries. This imbalance explains why there is no record of communal riots until after 1858 when the British crown directly assumed governance. How can there be a riot between a ruler and his fearful subjects? Riots can only take place when there is a semblance of balance.

The advent of the British signalled the defeat of those princes who were in power. Much more of India was ruled by Muslim *nawabs* than by Hindu *rajas*. The Mughal emperor was the titular head of the country; even the Marathas acknowledged him as such. The defeat was complete and formal when the rebellion or Mutiny of 1857 failed. As the British became rulers, Muslims as well as Hindus became subjects. Thus equality between the two communities was established for the first time. For the Hindus, it was a great relief that they had ceased to be either *zimmis* or *jaziya* payers. The British rulers were impartial umpires between the two communities.

These are facts. Yet, the myth of divide and rule was created. Evidently, neither British scholars nor rulers were able to nip it in the bud. They certainly could not have relished being accused of such an unscrupulous policy. This indicates that there is yet another myth: that our history has been written with bias, only because the British had it written while they ruled the country. They did intervene and favoured positions that served British interests. Our own scholars and politicians played their part in arriving at twisted historical conclusions. And here, the major responsibility must lie with anti-Hindus.

Maulana Muhammad Ali, who was the principal lieutenant of Mahatma Gandhi during his *satyagraha* campaign of 1920-21, refused to join him in the second campaign in 1930. At a meeting of the All India Muslim Conference in Bombay in April 1930, attended by over 20,000 Muslims, he bluntly stated: *"We refuse to join Mr Gandhi because his movement is not a movement for the complete independence of India but for making the seventy millions of Indian Musalmans dependents of the Hindu Mahasabha*". The Maulana made no secret of the fact that the Muslims, as a whole, were guided by pan-Islamism. He told members of the Round Table Conference in London that Islam was not confined to India. "*I belong", said he, "to two circles of equal size but which are not concentric. One is India and the other is the Muslim world. We are not nationalists but supra-nationalists*". In his address as Congress President in 1923, Maulana Muhammad Ali reminded the audience that extraterritorial sympathies were a part of the quintessence of Islam, as stated by RC Majumdar in *History of the Freedom Movement in India*, Volume III, Firma KL Mukhopadhyay, Calcutta 1977.

As is well known, Muhammad Ali and his brother Shaukat Ali, were followers of Mahatma Gandhi when he led the Khilafat movement to protect the throne of the Sultan of Turkey and the caliphate of all Sunni Muslims in the world. They lost all interest in Gandhi when, in 1924, Kemal Ataturk, the Turkish general, exiled the sultan and abolished the Khilafat.

Now read a few highlights from the "Lal Ishtihar" or the Red Pamphlet written by one Ibrahim Khan of Mymensingh district in East Bengal early in the 20th century; refer to page 108 of *Struggle for Freedom* by RC Majumdar, Bharatiya Vidya Bhawan, Bombay, 1988.

> Ye Musalmans! Arise, awake! Do not read in the same schools with Hindus. Do not buy anything from a Hindu shop. Do not touch any article manufactured by Hindu hands. Do not give any employment to a Hindu. Do not accept any degrading office under a Hindu. You are ignorant. But if you acquire knowledge you can at once send all Hindus to *jahannum* (hell). You form the majority of the population of this province. Among the cultivators also you form the majority. It is agriculture that is the source of wealth. The Hindu has no wealth of his own and has made himself rich only by despoiling you of your wealth. If you become sufficiently enlightened, then the Hindus will starve and soon become Mohammedans. Hindus are very selfish. As the progress of Mohammedans is inimical to the self-aggrandisement of Hindus, the latter will always oppose Mohammedan progress for their selfish ends. Be united in boycotting Hindus. What dire mischief have they not done to us! They have robbed us of honour and wealth. They have deprived us of our daily bread. And now they are going to deprive us of our very life.

Evidently, these are not the ravings of a normal person. Yet the depth of emotion is reflective of the deep divide between the two communities. British manipulation to divide Indians could not be compared to such venom, nor could any administration responsible for law and order possibly encourage such emotions. This does not mean that the British did not take tactical advantage of the differences, in order to sustain their rule. The point that is being made is that the divide was old and deep and the British were only the beneficiaries.

Decades have passed since the British left the sub-continent. Yet the tension between the two communities continues, between India and Pakistan, between India and Bangladesh and between the Hindus and Muslims. Why? Because, as Professor S Abid Husain has lucidly explained in *The National Culture of India,* (National Book Trust, 1972):

> "Like other Indian communities and most Asian peoples, while honouring as sacred, values of patriotism and loyalty to the state. Muslims are unanimous in rejecting what Western nations explicitly believe in the priority of country or state over religion."

A British view of the schism between the two communities is provided by Sir Percival Griffiths, ICS, in his book *The British Impact on India,* (Macdonald & Company Limited, London; 1952).

"India stood sharply divided between Hindus and Muslims. The feelings between them were much what could be expected since one community had been dominant and the other subject and often though not always oppressed. What is today called communal dissension was thus the permanent and inevitable legacy of centuries of Muslim rule."

Tracts on Partition

I

Gandhi-Jinnah Talks 1944 – On Partition

ON AUGUST 9, Gandhi was incarcerated in the wake of his 'Quit India' call to the British rulers. Two years later, when he was released, he wrote to Jinnah. His proposal was to meet and discuss with the Qaid-e-Azam the Partition of India. Jinnah replied that soon after he returned from his Kashmir holiday the two of them could meet in Bombay, which they did over a fortnight in September 1944. The meetings were held at Marble House on Malabar Hill. What was discussed was confirmed by letter by both the leaders. Fortunately therefore, first-hand records of what the two leaders talked are available and reproduced as part of the annexure to this volume. Incidentally, Gandhi addressed his letters to Jinnah as "*My dear Qaid-e-Azam*". Jinnah however, did not reciprocate by starting his letters with the word "Mahatma": They were begun with "*Dear Mr Gandhi*".

The central thrust of Jinnah's thinking was that Hindus and Muslims were so different that they could not coexist within the same country. He had put forward his views in detail in his presidential address delivered at Lahore on March 22, 1940. He was saying the same thing again at Marble House. India needs to be partitioned into now what is called Pakistan for the Muslims and Hindustan for the Hindus. This vivisection of the country must be done before, repeat, prior to the departure of the British. Partition first, Independence later. On the other hand, Gandhi preferred Independence first, Partition later. His contention was: let the foreigners depart for once; thereafter, like brothers, we can divide our country.

Neither Gandhi nor Jinnah budged from their respective positions, and therefore, the Marble House series of meetings ended. On the morrow of the Pakistan Resolution in March 1940, Gandhi had protested: "Partition over my dead body". In 1941, he had conceded to a journalist that every community had a right to self-determination. In 1942, Gandhi went to jail, in 1944, he conceded Partition in principle although after the British rulers left India.

II

Stern Reckoning

Stern Reckoning: A Survey of the Event leading up to and following the partition of India by Gopal Das Khosla, Barrister-at-law, Puisne Judge, East Punjab High Court:

Mortal Prudence, handmaid of divine Providence,
hath inscrutable reckoning with Fate and Fortune
We sail a changeful sea through halcyon days and storm,
and when the ship laboureth, our steadfast purpose
trembles like as the compass in a binnacle
Our stability is but balance, and wisdom lies
in masterful administration of the unforeseen

Robert Bridges
—Testament of Beauty 1916

Exodus

The Muslim League demand for Pakistan was based on the hypothesis that Hindus and Muslims constitute two separate nations, each entitled to a separate and exclusive homeland where they would be free to develop their culture, tradition, religion and polity On any other ground, the partition of the country and the setting up of a separate independent State for the Muslims would have been indefensible But the two-nation theory brought the problem of minorities into greater prominence than ever before, and Partition, instead of offering a solution, made it even more difficult and more complicated.

No matter where the line of demarcation was drawn, there would be Hindus, Muslims and Sikhs on either side of it, in a majority or in a substantial minority, and, whatever be the geographical boundaries of Pakistan, large numbers of Hindus and Sikhs would, overnight, become aliens and foreigners in their own homes Mr Jinnah made desperate efforts to evade the issue by promising protection and rights of citizenship to the minorities, but the nature of his demand was wholly inconsistent with these promises. How could millions of foreigners acquire rights of citizenship and equal status with the nationals of Pakistan? And if they could, why divide India? Why not let Muslims continue as nationals of India? Mr Jinnah could find no answer to these questions and he was finally compelled to suggest an exchange of population. This was such a fantastic idea that he referred to it, first, in a vague and hesitating manner, as if he were doing no more than throwing out a feeler to watch the reactions it brought forth. All he said was:

"It IS possible that there will have to be exchange of population if it can be done on a purely voluntary basis."* No one took Mr Jinnah seriously and, for a year, very little was said about the possibility contemplated by him To the Muslim League, however, it was a matter of great urgency as it offered a complete answer to the opponents of Pakistan. Exchange on a voluntary basis was an impossibility. The non-Muslims of the Punjab, North-West Frontier Province, Sindh and Bengal could never consent to leave their lands, the industry and commerce they had built up with their money and labour, and become beggars and nomads to satisfy a whim of Mr Jinnah's nor would the Muslims of the United Provinces, Bombay, Madras, Bihar and Central Provinces be willing to abandon their native soil, give up everything they owned and made life worth living, and migrate to distant lands. Human beings take moral and cultural roots in the soil where they live and prosper for generations and the ties that bind them to the native village and town are not easily severed. The dream of exchanging populations on a voluntary basis was impossible to realise and the Muslim League had to find another way of resolving the difficulty.

The Calcutta experiment did not produce very satisfactory results but it achieved a certain measure of success, in that large

---

* Mr Jinnah's Interview to the Special Correspondent of the Associated Press of India on December 10, 1945, published in the *Dawn* of 12 December 1945.

numbers of non-Muslims were intimidated into leaving their homes even though for a temporary period.* The experience gained, proved useful in Noakhali and Tippera. A change of tactics, better organisation and more favourable conditions for women, and conversion wholesale to Islam. This was a more effective way of dealing with the minorities and obviated the difficulties involved in an exchange of population. The events in Bihar compelled many Muslims to leave the province and seek shelter in Sindh, and the question of exchange arose once again. It was now taken up by the League leaders and put forward in all seriousness and with all the vehemence at their command. They became more and more uncompromising on this issue and answered all criticism by uttering scarcely veiled threats, and predicted a horrible doom for those who disagreed with them.

On November 25, 1946, Mr Jinnah, addressing a Press Conference at Karachi expressed the opinion that "the authorities, both Central and Provincial, should take up immediately the question of exchange of population."* This brought forth a storm of protest from non-Muslims all over India. Sir Chimanlal Setalvad, the Liberal leader, described the idea as "hopelessly impracticable." Sardar Swaran Singh said, "the Sikhs in the Punjab would not tolerate any move

* *Dawn*, November 26, 1046.
Dawn, December 3, 1946.
Dawn, December 4, 1946.
Dawn, December 19, 1946.

to this end." Sardar Patel, addressing the Nagpur University Convocation, characterised Mr Jinnah's proposal as "absurd" and one which "can never materialise." The Muslim League leaders, on the other hand, expressed their wholehearted approval of the scheme. Khan Iftikhar Hussain Khan of Mamdot declared, with great enthusiasm, that "the exchange of population offered a most practical solution of the multifarious problems" of the Muslims. "We are not going to ask Sardar Patel or Dr Khare for it, but we will get it by our own inherent strength. The exchange of population will wipe out the most important argument against Pakistan which has been persistently fired from the Congress armoury."* The frank avowal and the unabashed threat, implicit in this utterance, were hardly calculated to inspire confidence in the minorities.

Pir llahi Bux, the Sindh leader said, he "welcomed an exchange of population for the safety of minorities" as such an exchange would put an end to all communal disturbances. Sir Evan Jenkins, the Governor of the Punjab, observed that by advocating an exchange of population the Muslim League was thinking of forcibly driving away the Hindus from the Punjab. This brought forth a protest from Raja Ghaznafar Ali Khan. "This is certainly not so." he said, "the Muslim League will do everything possible to protect the minorities living in

* *Dawn*, November 26, 1046.
Dawn, December 3, 1946.
Dawn, December 4, 1946.
Dawn, December 19, 1946.

the Muslim majority areas and will even be prepared to give what help is possible for any plans of strengthening the sense of security among Hindus where they happen to be living as a scattered minority." But, lest his professions of sympathy were misconstrued, he added darkly. "After what has happened, the present position cannot be accepted with equanimity and minorities which are too scattered and helpless owing to the smallness of their numbers must not be left as a tempting prey to those who can arrange organised lawlessness."*

Sir Feroze Khan Noon had already threatened to re-enact the murderous orgies of Changez Khan and Halaqu Khan if the non-Muslims took up a refractory altitude. Everything was now ready and, in the month of January 1947, the agitation against the Punjab Coalition Ministry was started. how it promoted lawlessness and utter disregard of authority, and provided an opportunity for the Muslim League to organise their forces and rehearse the great *putsch* which would solve the problem of minorities once and for all. The agitation culminated in the resignation of the Khizar Ministry and when the prospect of a League Government provoked the Sikh leaders into giving vent to their anger and fears in somewhat stupid and boastful words, their utterances were made the excuse for launching a bloody assault on non-Muslim life and property.

The Sikhs had opposed the Partition of India with even greater vigour than the Hindus, because they felt that as a

---

* Speech at the Convention of the Muslim League legislators on April 9, 1946.

community they could only expect disaster in Pakistan. It was, therefore, against the Sikhs that the spear-point of the Muslim League attack was first aimed. In the March riots, the Sikhs of Rawalpindi faced annihilation and large numbers of them left the district. Within a few weeks almost the entire Sikh population (save those who were killed or converted) had migrated from the district. On a somewhat smaller scale a movement of the Hindus from Multan, Jhelum, Attock and Bahawalpur also took place. Some of these non-Muslims went back when peaceful conditions were restored during the months of April, May, June and July.*

* Stern Reckoning: *A Survey of the Events Leading Up to and Following the Partition of India* Book by G D Khosla.
First published in 1949 in the aftermath of Partition, and now available for the first time in paperback, Stern Reckoning documents in great detail the riots, massacres, casualty figures, and political occurrences that added up to the division of India into two countries, India and Pakistan.
Originally published: 1949.
Author: G D Khosla.
Publisher: OUP India; Reprint edition (22 February 1990).

III

Subcontinental Ummah is One

Dawn of 23 March 2002

Lest what is presented in this book appears to be old, obsolete or *passe*, it is necessary to see how the well known Karachi daily *Dawn* celebrated Pakistan Day on 23 March, 2002. Incidentally, Pakistan Day is an annual celebration of the 'Pakistan resolution' passed by the Muslim League at its Lahore session of 1940. That was when an open and official demand was made by the League for the bifurcation of the country and the creation of Pakistan.

The extent have the sentiments of the Pakistani intelligentsia remained faithful to the inspiration generated by the League leaders led by Qaid-e-Azam Jinnah who died in September,

1948 is uncanny. The Pakistanis still appear to be loyal to his thoughts and concepts. If any differences or disagreements with Jinnah have been expressed, they are by Indian Muslims like Dr Rafiq Zakaria who either chose to remain stay put in India or just could not emigrate. Even a scholar of the stature of Dr Zakaria has taken the best part of half a century to realise and protest that Jinnah had done enormous damage to the community which remained in Hindustan.

Janab Sharif al Mujahid has written the lead article in the supplement of the same edition reminding the reader of Jinnah's concept of Pakistan. There are in all eleven articles, none of which expresses any difference of opinion with Jinnah's dream, with the bounties that the creation of Pakistan showered upon the Muslim *ummah*. Remarkably, in all the articles, the underlying presumption is that the *ummah* includes all the Muslims of the subcontinent. There is no separate mention of either Indian Muslims or Bangladeshis or the *mohajirs*.

That the *mohajirs* are ill treated in Karachi, or the rest of Sindh or anywhere else in Pakistan would appear to be largely a myth or at least an exaggeration. There must be some legitimate grievances, but to say that they are because of their being *mohajirs* and not the original sons of the soil does not seem to make sense. Had it been so, how is it that the founder of Pakistan, the Qaid-e-Azam, his successor as leader Nawabzada Liaquat AIi Khan who was born in Kamal, in what is now Haryana, Ibrahim Ismail Chundrigar, one of the prime ministers who followed, hailed from Godhra in Gujarat, were all accepted despite being *mohajirs?* The longest serving President was General Zia-ul-Haq hailed from Jalandhar and was educated at St. Stephens College, Delhi. General Pervez Musharraf belonged to Delhi before his immediate family migrated to Pakistan. Had the *mohajirs* been unwelcome, surely so many of them would not have adorned the crown of Pakistan!

To reiterate, the *Dawn* supplement gives the impression that in the Pakistani mind, there is no segregation of the sub-continental *ummah* on the basis of national borders, as seen in the second paragraph of the first article:

> For Muslims in pre-Partition India, with their deep horizontal, vertical, regional and linguistic cleavages Islam alone could serve as a broad political platform a la Karl Deutsch (Nationalism and Social Communism) typology, to gather incrementally all the Muslims under the all embracing Pakistan canopy.

Mujahid quotes Allama Iqbal:

> Had not only furnished the Muslims of the subcontinent with those basic emotions and loyalties which gradually unify scattered individuals and groups, but had also worked as a people building force, transforming them progressively into a well defined people. The unity of Indian Islam, so far as it had achieved unity, may first and foremost be attributed to (what Montgomery Watt calls) a dynamic image, the image or idea of the charismatic community.

Mujahid continues:

> This explains how scattered, though they were across

> the length and breadth of the subcontinent in varying proportions, they had yet developed the will to live as a nation on the basis, in Toynbean terminology, of their social heritage. This national will in turn provided the Indian Muslims with the intellectual and political satisfaction for claiming a distinct nationalism for themselves.

Continuing, Mujahid writes:

> The demand for Pakistan was, thus the result, not primarily of racial, linguistic or territorial nationalism, although these factors could by no means be brushed aside, but chiefly of religious nationalism.

He goes on to quote Jinnah:

> We wish our people to develop to the fullest our spiritual, cultural, economic, social and political life in a way that we think best and which is in consonance with our own ideals and according to the genius of our people.

Prof Sharif al Mujahid, in order to show that the demand for Pakistan had the mandate of Muslims across the subcontinent says:

> The Muslim League, despite all odds, swept the polls in the 1945-46 general elections, bagging 75 percent of the popular vote and 85 percent of the Muslim seats.

The article goes on to answer the question again as to what was Jinnah's concept of Pakistan. He quotes from a message given by Jinnah on 18 June 1945. It was to the Frontier NSF (Northern Security Force) and it talks about Muslim ideology which has to be preserved, which has come to us as a precious gift and treasure.

What was this Muslim ideology was again best defined by the Qaid-e-Azam himself in one of his contemporary speeches:

> The Hindus and Muslims belong to two different religious philosophies, social customs, literature... indeed they belong to two different civilisations which are based mainly on conflicting ideas and conceptions. Their aspects on life and of life are different. It is quite clear that Hindus and Mussalmans derive their inspiration from different sources of history. They have different epics, different heroes and different episodes. Very often the hero of one is a foe of the other and likewise their victories and defeats overlap.
>
> The credit of having created a new state and founding a Darul- Islam must go to Mohammed Ali Jinnah. It is probable that without his leadership the Muslim League might have been outmanoeuvred at the time out of its demand for a Muslim homeland. No State is perfect and Pakistan must have many a fault. Nevertheless, it is a land where the writ of *sharia* runs. What this means for a devout Muslim or a *Momin* is seldom appreciated by a Hindu mind which has never identified the state or a government with his own faith. Religion is something that the Hindu does not have. He has faith only in the *paramatma* and his *dharma* which is a combination of morality, duty and devotion. Over and above all this, he has an explanation of life, but nowhere is there any mention of politics or government.

In contrast, one face of Islam is that of a political party, the Party of Allah, and its name is Hizbullah, as lucidly explained by Maulana Abul Kalam Azad while writing in his journal

Al Hilal during 1913. Islam is not merely a faith. It is a total prescription for life and living. Prophet Muhammad was a versatile genius in every sphere of life that he lived. He traded and made money, he was a general who led the army and made conquests. He was a king, to begin with, of Medina and later large tracts of Arabia including Mecca. He was a happy householder with the gift of many children *et al.* The message or the *paigham* he delivered was comprehensive and covered almost all aspects of life. For the Hindu mind to understand this is not easy.

However prosperous, successful and personally happy, however powerful or famous the Indian Muslim might be, he cannot quite attain complete fulfilment unless his life is allowed to blossom in a garden of Dar-ul-Islam.

IV

Dr Rajendra Prasad on India Divided, 1946

After all the attempts to solve the Hindu-Muslim problem up to the Simla Conference in July 1945, other developments have taken place which is relevant. In the course of the discussions which Mahatma Gandhi had with Mr Jinnah in 1944, it emerged more or less clearly for the first time that demarcating the areas which were to be included in the Muslim Zones, the units for considering whether they had a majority of Muslims in them were to be the Provinces and not Districts or any other smaller areas, need to be determined. The League and its leaders had persistently refused to give any indication of their mind on this point till Sri C Rajagopalachariar put forward his formula providing that a commission shall be appointed for demarcating contiguous districts in the North-

West and East of India, wherein the Muslim populations were in absolute majority and practically forced Mr Jinnah to state to the representative of the *News Chronicle* of London on 4th October 1944, that India should be divided into two sovereign parts of Pakistan and Hindustan by the recognition of the whole of the North-West Frontier Province, Baluchistan, Sind, Punjab, Bengal and Assam as sovereign Muslim territories as they now stand.

In another interview to the representative of the *Daily Worker* of London on 5th October 1944, he said: "To understand the Pakistan demand in its full significance, it is to be borne in mind that the six Provinces, viz. the NWFP, Baluchistan, Sind, and the Punjab in the North-West, and Bengal and Assam in the North-East of this sub-continent, have a population of 70 million Muslims and the total population of Muslims would not be less than 70 per cent." At a Press Conference which he gave after the termination of the Gandhi-Jinnah talks, Mr Jinnah referred a questioner to the Lahore Resolution which stated that the division should be on the basis of the present boundaries of the six Provinces, i.e. the NWFP, the Punjab, Sind, Bengal, Assam and Baluchistan, subject to territorial adjustments that might be necessary. He emphasized the words subject to and explained that territorial adjustments did not apply to one side only but to both sides, Hindustan and Pakistan, making it clear that the question of demarcating or defining the boundaries can be taken up later in the same way as the question of boundaries arising between two nations is solved. It is thus made clear that the units are to be the Provinces and not any smaller areas like the commissionerships or districts, taluks or sub-divisions. One point was still left vague, viz. the question of territorial adjustments. We shall see later how that is being interpreted now.

We may notice here Mr Jinnah's statement to the representative of the *Daily Worker* that Pakistan so defined as to comprise the six Provinces mentioned above will have a population of 70 million Muslims and the total population of Muslims would not be less than 70 per cent. Mr Jinnah evidently does not believe in figures and seems to think that arithmetic no less than geography and the history of a thousand years can be controlled and altered by mere assertion of a palpably untenable proposition.

The tables of population given in another part of this book will show that the total population of the North-Western Zone comprising the four Provinces of the NWFP, Baluchistan, Sind and the Punjab would be 3,64,93,525 out of which the number of Muslims would be 2,26,53,294, or 62.07 per cent. Similarly the total population of the Eastern Zone comprising the Provinces of Assam and Bengal in their entirety will be 7,05,11,258 out of which the Muslims would be only 3,64.47,913, or 51.69 per cent. If the two zones are taken together, their total population will come to 10,70,4,783 of which the Muslims would be 5,91,01,207, or 55.23 per cent. We see that the population of the Muslims in the two zones taken together is only 59 millions and not 70 millions as stated by Mr Jinnah and that its proportion to the total population of the two Zones is only 55.23 per cent and not 70 per cent as claimed by him.

Some clarification is now available of the 'territorial adjustments' referred to above. In an interview to Mr Donald Edwards of the BBC Mr Jinnah was asked about the difficulty of forming a Pakistan State out of the two areas, one in the North-East of India, one in the North-West, nearly a thousand miles apart, with a Hindu corridor dividing them. Mr Jinnah replied: "When you travel from Britain to the other parts of the British Commonwealth, you pass through foreign territory-Suez Canal, for instance. It is all done by amicable arrangement. We travel from the Muslim areas of the North-East to the Muslim areas of the North-West across this so-called Hindu corridor without any difficulty today. Why should that arrangement not continue? The Hindus must not be allowed to put difficulties in the way of a State that wants to be their neighbour in a friendly way. They must not be allowed to close the doors of communication between the Muslims of North-West India and the Muslims of North-East. This must be one of the terms of the treaty."

This statement, by the way, makes the two Zones in the North-East and North-West of India into one single Muslim State. It would be recalled that the Lahore Resolution of the League passed in March 1940 said that the areas in which the Muslims are in a majority in the North-Western and Eastern Zones of India should be grouped to constitute independent

States and not one single State. Mr Jinnah now claims that not only should the two zones constitute one single State but that the Hindu State must also provide a corridor of nearly a thousand miles between the two Muslim Zones. He mentions that there is free passage between the Eastern and the Western Zones today and asks – why should that arrangement not continue? The simple answer to that question is that the two zones and the intervening territory are today included in one single State and as such they have not only a free passage as between them but are under one Central Government with its headquarters at Delhi. After separation the two States of Pakistan and Hindustan will be independent sovereign States and there can be no question of one independent State allowing passage through its territory to another independent State to enable the latter to have a land route to one of its outlying parts.

In the same interview, Mr Jinnah was questioned as to why Assam with its huge Hindu population should be part of Pakistan. He replied: 'There is no other way of fitting Assam anywhere except in Pakistan.' Evidently Mr Jinnah thinks that if Bengal is included in Pakistan, Assam is cut off from the rest of India and it must therefore be included in the Eastern Zone of Pakistan. Now, Assam will be cut off from Hindustan only if the districts of Jalpaiguri and Darjeeling with a Muslim population of 23 per cent and 2.4 per cent respectively and the Hindu State of Cooch Behar with 62 per cent Hindus in its population are included in the Muslim Zone. Logic and fair play have no place when the question to be considered is, which areas are to be included within the sovereign Pakistan State. Districts with an overwhelming Hindu population, both in the Punjab and in Bengal and Assam, must be included within Pakistan because today they happen to be parts of Provinces which are claimed to be Muslim Zones. Hindus must not be allowed to stand in the way of a corridor being provided between the two Muslim Zones. Assam should be included in the Eastern Zone because it would be cut off from Hindustan. It must be cut off from Hindustan because no corridor can be allowed by the Muslim State to join Assam with Hindustan through the districts which are overwhelmingly Hindu in population. Evidently it is a case of heads we win, tails you lose.

Another point to be considered is Mr Suhrawardy's, the Prime Minister of the League Ministry of Bengal, claims that not only the whole of Bengal and Assam but also the districts of Singhbhum, Manbhum, Santhal Parganas and Purnea of Bihar should be included within Pakistan. They will, of course, form part of the Eastern Zone. Pakistan will then be in a position to say that most of the iron and copper ore, most of the coal and the oil and many of the other metals that are to be found in India are within Pakistan. People have been at pains to point out that Pakistan will be lacking in most of these essential commodities which cannot be dispensed with in any independent State. Mr Suhrawardy answers by claiming that the areas which possess these commodities must be included within Pakistan. They will thus be made self-sufficient in this respect. It, of course, does not matter that they are not included within the Provinces claimed for Pakistan and the Muslim population in them is very small, only 18.12 per cent of the total population.

TABLE LIV
Muslim and non-Muslim population in the- North-Western and Eastern Zones with our Districts of Bihar added

	Total Population	Muslim Population	Percentage of Muslim Population	Non-Muslim Population	Percentage of Muslim Population
North-Western Zone	3,64,93,525	2,26,53,294	62.07	1,38,40,231	37.92
Bengal and Assam	7,05,11,258	3,64,47,913	51.69	3,40,63,345	48.30
Total of NW Zoneand Bangal & Assam	**10,70,04,783**	**5,91,01,207**	**55.23**	**4,79,03,576**	**44.76**
Bihar Districts					
Purnea	23,90,105	9,76,048	40.84	14,14,057	59.16
Santhal Pargana	22,34,497	2,62,836	11.76	19,71,661	88.24
Manbhum	20,32,146	1,32,234	6.51	18,99,912	93.49
Singhbhum	11,44,717	43,233	3.77	11,01,484	81.87
Total of Bihar Districts	**78,01,465**	**14,14,351**	**18.12**	**63,87,114**	**81.87**
Grand Total of NW Zone, Bengal, Assam and four Districts of Bihar	11,48,06,248	6,05,15,558	52.17	5,42,90,690	47.28

It may also be pointed out in passing that in the population of the Eastern Zone, as it will be if these districts are included within it, the Muslims will be actually in a minority of 48.34 per cent, and whatever justification there is for claiming a separate independent State of Muslims on the basis of their being in a majority in the population of an area ceases to exist after this territorial adjustment. Even if we take the total population of the two Zones together the proportion of the Muslim population will be reduced from a small majority of 55.23 per cent to a nominal majority of 2.71 per cent. Thus, we now know what is meant by territorial adjustment which, according to Mr Jinnah must be on both sides. Hindustan must give and Pakistan must take.

Another question has been engaging public attention ever since the two nation theory was propounded. All Muslims being one nation by reason of their religion alone irrespective of any other considerations like the territory they inhabit, the language they speak, etc. The question naturally arises what would be the position and status of the Muslims who will be left in Hindustan, which according to the League proposal will be a Hindu State.

Mr Jinnah, on being asked what he proposed for those areas where the Muslims are in a minority replied in the course of the interview referred to above: 'Those areas, like Madras for instance, will .have a Hindu Government and the Muslim minority there will have three courses open to them: they may accept citizenship of the State in which they are, they can remain there as foreigners or they can come to Pakistan. I will welcome them. There is plenty of room. But it is for them to decide.' Mr Jinnah accepts the position that the Muslims who are citizens of India today will, after Partition, cease to be citizens of Hindustan and therefore they will have three alternatives to choose from. Let us examine these three alternatives.

The first alternative is that they may accept citizenship in the State which they are in. It may be pointed out that citizenship can be acquired by a foreigner in a State only under rules made for that purpose by the State concerned. It is open to any State which is independent to regulate and control its own population and to lay down restrictions on foreigners acquiring citizenship and even to prohibit it altogether. The history of the British Dominions like South Africa, Canada and Australia, which are all members of the British Commonwealth and the Empire, to which India also belongs, and which owe allegiance to the same King-Emperor to whom Indians are in law required to owe allegiance, shows how they have successfully and effectively prevented Indians from acquiring the rights of citizenship. The United States of America also regulates immigration and does not permit any and every foreigner to acquire the right of citizenship simply because the foreigner wishes to have that right. So, if Hindustan is to be really a free and sovereign State, it will have the same right to regulate its citizenship and to lay down rules for and even to prohibit acquisition of the rights of citizenship by foreigners. It will not lie with the Muslims left in Hindustan to become its citizens unless Hindustan permits it. Mr Jinnah, of course, assumes that Hindus must not be allowed to put difficulties in their way.

The second alternative is that they can remain there as foreigners. Here again he makes the same assumption. Hindustan like any other independent state will not be bound to allow foreigners to remain its territory, particularly when they happen to be in such large numbers as the Muslims will be. It is also worth remembering that an independent state may regulate and even prohibit the acquisition of property, particularly immovable property, by foreigners within its territory. We have the illustration once again of South Africa before our eyes.

The third alternative is that the Musalmans who will be left in Hindustan can go to Pakistan. This, of course, is legally possible. Every foreigner is entitled to leave the foreign state and to go to his own State unless he is accused of a crime for which he is to face trial in the foreign State. The Musalmans of Hindustan can leave Hindustan if they so desire but they cannot carry away with them their lands and houses, even if they are allowed and are in a position to take away their movables like cash, jewellery, cattle and furniture. Hindustan will not be bound to give any compensation for what they leave behind. They would have migrated out of Hindustan of their own free will by reason of their having adopted a foreign nationality. It is difficult to believe that the Muslims of Hindustan will choose this alternative of emigration from Hindustan. Their attachment to their lands and homes will make any such break most difficult, if not impracticable. The distance which they will, in many cases, have to travel before they can reach Pakistan will be immense and the consequent suffering will be unbearable. Last, though not least, the complete dislocation of their finances and economy which migration will involve will effectively prohibit any such enterprise. They will have, therefore, only the first two alternatives to choose from and there they will not be free to do so as the foreign State of Hindustan will have an effective and determining hand in the matter.

All these considerations which arise out of the two nation theory do not appear to trouble the protagonists of Pakistan. Mr Jinnah now evidently accepts the position, which indeed cannon be questioned, that the Muslims in Hindustan will have the status of foreigners or aliens and will, therefore, be subject to the same disabilities that a foreigner suffers from. The same consideration might not apply to Hindus and non-Muslims who will be left in Pakistan, as they do not claim to be members of another nation and as such citizens of another state. But, in any case, even if they are treated as foreigners or aliens, the difference in their position will be that foreign citizenship would have been forced upon them against their will, while in the case of Muslims, it would have been chosen by them of their own free will with their eyes open and indeed against the wishes and in face of the opposition of the Hindus and other non-Muslims.

This addendum will not be complete without reference to general elections to the Assemblies both Central and Provincial. The Muslim League attained, phenomenal success in the elections to the Central Assembly and secured all the seats reserved for Musalmans. It may, however, be pointed out that the Nationalist Muslims secured nearly one-fourth of the total votes polled as against the League. In Sindh they secured 32 per cent and in the Punjab 30 per cent of the total

Muslim votes cast. The NWFP sends only one representative to the Central Assembly who is returned by a joint electorate of Muslims and non-Muslims. So also does Delhi send one representative elected by a joint electorate. Both these places were captured by Muslim candidates who had been set up on behalf of the Congress.

At the Provincial elections the Muslim League had set up candidates for the seats reserved for Musalmans and there was contest in many of them between the League candidates on the one hand and other Muslim candidates set up by Jamait-ul-Ulema, the Momins, the Ahrars and other Nationalist Muslim organizations and some Independents on the other. The League secured the seats mentioned below in the Provinces claimed by the League for Pakistan and in which elections have been held. Baluchistan has no assembly at present and hence no elections.

TABLE LV
Analysis of Muslim Voting for Provincial Elections

Provinces	Seats Secured by League	Seats Secured by non-League Muslim	Votes for the League	Percentage for votes for the League	Votes secured by non-League Muslims	Percentage of votes non-League Muslims
NWFP	17	21	1,47,880	41.4	2,08,896	58.5
Sind	26	8	1,99,651	56.8	1,52,235	43.2
The Punjab	73	13	6,79,796	65.1	3,58,235	34.3
Assam	31	3	1,88,071	69.0	84,453	31.0

The Muslim League was unable to form ministries in the NWFP, the Punjab and Assam. In the NWFP and Assam, the Congress had an absolute majority in the Assembly and as such the Congress Party alone was in a position to form ministries and it was asked by the Governor to do so and it did. It may also be mentioned that in the NWFP not only had the Congress an absolute majority in the Provincial Assembly but it had also a majority from among the Muslim members in it. In the Sindh Assembly, the Congress alongwith the non-League Muslims had 29 members, the League had 28. There, were three Europeans, who declared themselves to be neutral in the matter of formation of the ministry. The Governor, however, chose to invite the League to form the ministry which it did and the ministry was able to function with the help of the three European members. The only other Province where the League has been able to form a ministry is Bengal.

The leaders of the League have, however, declared that they did not fight the elections with a view to forming ministries but for the larger and higher purpose of establishing Pakistan and they claim that the elections have shown that Musalmans are overwhelmingly in favour of Pakistan. The figures given above, however, show that in the North-West Frontier Province a majority of Musalmans is opposed to the Pakistan idea. In Sindh no less than 43 per cent and in the Punjab 34 per cent of Muslim voters are opposed to the League and Pakistan. In Assam, which is overwhelmingly non-Muslim, 31 per cent even of the Muslims are opposed to it. The figures for Bengal are not given because they were not available at the time of writing this. It is unnecessary to go into the figures of the other Provinces which are not claimed by the League for Pakistan and the opinion of Musalmans there can have significance only as being a vote in favour of the Musalmans of those Provinces being regarded as foreigners there. It may also be pointed out that it would be most unfair not to recognize the right of non-Muslims of the areas sought to be separated to express themselves on the question of separation. If their votes at the elections are counted along with those of the Musalmans who are opposed to Pakistan, it will be clear that the Provinces as a whole are opposed to Pakistan and the results of the Assembly elections far from being in favour of Pakistan, are opposed to it.

V

Mujeeb Censured Muslim League

In his book called *Islamic Influence on Indian Society*, published by Meenakshi Prakashan, Meerut, 1972, Professor M Mujeeb, former Vice-Chancellor of Jamia Millia, has analysed the reasons for the Partition and described the condition of the Muslims who remained in India. We have read in the last chapter what Maulana Abul Kalam Azad had feared in the years immediately preceding the bifurcation and how he was vindicated in the following ten years. Mujeeb assessed the state of the Muslims 25 years after the event. It is best to reproduce his words:

> At a party given during the UN General Assembly Session in 1949 I had the pleasure of being placed next to the Turkish representative. He looked at my name

> card, saw that I was a Muslim and at once asked. Are there still any Muslims in India? The impression then created does not yet seem to have been removed and it is believed that the subcontinent had been divided between Muslims and Hindus, with all Muslims on the one side and all Hindus on the other.

The impression of the Turkish representative that there might not be any Muslims left in India could be due to the fact that exchanges of population had taken place between Greece and Turkey as well as between Bulgaria and Turkey during the 1920s. He must not have realised that there was no such exchange in our subcontinent. As Mujeeb puts it:

> The reasons why India was partitioned is a painful subject not only for the Hindus, but for a vast number of Muslims, both in India and Pakistan. I do not propose to discuss here the reasons for the Partition. It is necessary to remember two facts because of their consequences. The Muslim League was the party which demanded the creation of Pakistan as 'a separate homeland for the Indian Muslims'. In the elections held early in 1946, which proved decisive, it secured 425 out of 492 seats reserved for Muslims in the Central and the different Provincial Legislatures. It could therefore be said, that Indian Muslims were overwhelmingly in favour of Pakistan ... It insisted that the right to 'a separate homeland for the Muslims, to be called Pakistan, should be conceded first.' The voting for Pakistan was thus a leap in the dark and can hardly be regarded as a considered move.

Mujeeb continues:

> It is significant in this connection that no outstanding persons or groups in Pakistan made any effective attempt to ensure the security of the Hindus or to enable those who did not wish to migrate to stay on. If they had done so, the lot of the Muslims, immediately after Partition would have been much easier. The decision in regard to exchange of populations applied only to Eastern and Western Punjab. A large proportion of the Hindus in the North West Frontier Province and in Sindh would have stayed on if they could. On the other hand, there would have been much less of immigration of the Hindus of East Pakistan into West Bengal and anti-Muslim sentiment in eastern and northern India would not have been constantly revived.

Mujeeb goes on:

> The security of Muslims in India has been endangered by these actively hostile elements, and by the attitude of the government of East Pakistan towards its Hindu citizens... The ideology of the Muslim League and the demand of a separate homeland for the Muslims was based on the assumption that the whole Muslim community possesses a common political and economic interest. But even a superficial consideration of the distribution of the Muslim community in the country and the many economic classes of which it is constituted would at once disprove this theory... There is still a Muslim League party in a southern state, but anywhere else in India a purely Muslim political party would not be able to achieve anything and would only antagonise the other communities.

VI

Zakaria Blames Jinnah

Dr Raflq Zakaria, in his book entitled *The Man who Divided India*, (Popular Prakashan. Mumbai, 200), has painted a dark picture. To some extent his version must be affected by his personal perspective which includes participation in politics. For the rest, his views are a result of Muslim disillusionment which grew over 29 years that elapsed between Mujeeb's book and Zakaria's study. Zakaria's work has been widely read by those interested in the subject. It is therefore sufficient to highlight by quoting from a few passages.

Let us first deal with the Indian Muslims; their story is heart-rending. I have detailed their plight in my book *The Widening Divide*, published by Penguin India. Suffice to say that in their religious frenzy and the fear of Hindu domination indoctrinated in them by Jinnah, they became blind to the possible consequences of Partition.

The Muslims of Bombay, UP and Bihar were the first to respond to the call of Jinnah for Partition and enthusiastically supported the movement for Pakistan. They became its vanguard. They were so fanatically charged by Jinnah's slogan of "Islam in danger" and frightened by the bogey of Hindu domination, constantly raised by him that they were easily misled. They failed to ask themselves: how could the creation of a State in the faraway North-West-consisting of half of Punjab, Sindh, the Frontier and Baluchistan and still further in the North-East-consisting of half of Bengal and a part of Assam-provide any security to the rest of the Muslims living in Hindu-dominated regions and spread over cities, towns and villages? No sooner did this realisation dawn on them, they asked Jinnah on the eve of the formation of Pakistan: "What is to happen to us who are being left behind?" He assured them that if any harm came to them, Pakistan would retaliate against the Hindus under its control.

But he could not have been serious about that for he must have known that after the hate campaign he had unleashed against the Hindus, few of them would have dared to stay on in his Pakistan. And they did not; they fled in the most excruciating circumstances-many died on the way, the rest reached India with nothing... This is the result of Jinnah's politics: he had vowed that he would provide the Muslims a separate homeland to free them from Hindu domination. But what has really happened is that they have been permanently enslaved, two-thirds of them to the Hindus and the remaining one-third which constitute Pakistan to the power-brokers and drug dealers.

VII

NV Gadgil on Nehru-Liaquat Pact, 1950

Dr NV Gadgil was a senior member of Jawaharlal Nehru's first cabinet. In Gadgil's words: "I have already described (ear;ier) how systematically Pakistan drove out its Hindus and how they encouraged Bengali Muslims to enter and occupy some areas in Assam. The Indian Government took no notice of these. On the other hand, Nehru was greatly annoyed when once Vallabhbhai suggested mutual exchange of Hindu and Muslim populations and a proportionate division of land between India and Pakistan. Such an exchange would have been beneficial in the long run..... Thousands of Muslims who had gone to Pakistan returned and were given back their properties. The Hindus received no such justice. It is true that Hindu refugees became objects of charity and received monetary assistance.

But the self-respect and religious faith for which they had made such sacrifices were not honoured.... And we overlooked in the past many of their (Muslims') transgressions because they were a minority. Our difficulties today sprang from this weakness. This temperament of Nehru made simple problems complex.

1949 saw such unspeakable atrocities against Hindus in East Pakistan that it became almost imperative to go to their help. The cabinet discussed the situation at great length and decided that some action should be initiated.

But Nehru did not want it. The Prime Minister of Pakistan Liaquat Ali came to Delhi in March 1950, had discussions with Nehru and one fine morning at 10 o'clock Nehru placed before the cabinet a draft of his agreement with him. I am not sure if Vallabhbhai was consulted before the draft was agreed to. The final two paragraphs in the agreement accepted the principle of reservation for Muslims in proportion to their population in all the services and representative benches in the constituent states of India and similar provisions were suggested for Central Government also. I said,'These two paragraphs nullify the whole philosophy of the Congress. The country had to pay the price of division as a result of its acceptance of separate electorates. You are asking it to drink the same poison again. This is a betrayal of the last forty years of history.' Nehru was displeased. I said: 'These two paragraphs must go lock, stock and barrel.' Nehru replied in anguish: '*I have agreed to this with Liaquat Ali Khan.*' When the cabinet met the next day, the last two paragraphs were omitted."

VIII

Durga Das Basu on Indian Muslims

In the international sphere, the minority problem arose when the population of a country came to be directed *against their will*, by external circumstances, such as war, to another country so that the divided community which became a minority in another country needed safeguards to save them from ethnic extinction. On the other hand, the Muslims obtained the Partition of India on their own demand on the basis of the 'Two-Nation' theory, and even after that Partition, a section of the Muslim community preferred to remain in India out of their own choice. Nobody compelled them to remain in divided India (which was a creation of theirs).

When they opted to remain in divided India, they did not

enter into any covenant with the Government of divided India. No observation of Maulana Azad can be enforced as a legal covenant in an international court.

The leaders of divided India incorporated in their Draft Constitution certain safeguards for minorities, notwithstanding the Partition, because they refused to concede on principle, that the Muslims in India constituted a separate Nation. That India constituted one Nation whose unity and integrity must be maintained was proclaimed in the very Preamble of the Draft Constitution of divided India. The Muslims who opted to remain in divided India did so with their eyes open to this Preamble and the safeguards for minorities included in that Draft.

These have ultimately been embodied in Articles. 25-30 of the Constitution as finally adopted in 1949. Hence, all the safeguards in Article. 27 of the International Covenant are already embodied in the Constitution of India, viz., the right (a) to enjoy their own culture [Articles. 29-30]; (b) to profess and practice their own religion [Article. 25 (1)]; and (c) to use their own language [Article. 29 (6)1. If any of these rights are infringed, any member of the minority community can legally enforce them in the national courts under Article. 32 or 226.1

However the Muslims and their advocates are not contended with this. They want things beyond what is already contained in the Constitution adopted by the 'People of India', which included the Muslims who opted to remain in India, e.g., to eliminate or scrap Article. 44 of the Constitution which enjoins the Government of India to make a common civil code for all the people of India.

The highest Tribunal of the land which is also to abide by Article. 44, by reason of Article. 36, read with Article. 12, has been repeatedly reminding the Government of India of their duty to implement Article. 44, when half a century has elapsed since the adoption of the Constitution.

As against this, what covenant will a journalist produce before an international forum to establish the case of those who are still fostering the ghost of the 'Two-Nation' theory, to disintegrate the unity of India, and to override the highest law of the land ?

On this point, I can do no better than to quote from a recent Supreme Court judgment [Mudgal v *Union of India*, A 1995 SC 1531 (para 3.5)].

"Those who preferred to remain in India after the Partition, fully knew that the Indian leaders did not believe in the two-nation or three-nation theory and that in the Indian Republic there was to be only one Nation – the Indian Nation – *and no community could claim to remain a separate entity on the basis of religion."* [See also *Bommai* v *Union of India*, A 1994 SC 1918 (para 21) – 9 – Judges]

No dogmatism of a journalist, coloured by a communal vision, can demolish the foregoing observation of the highest tribunal which is founded on patent history.

It is an amazing evidence of the foresight of the Indian leaders that even though the International Covenant on Civil and Political Rights was made some two decades later, they anticipated the contents of Article. 27 of the International

Covenant and embodied them in the Draft Constitution. But that cannot confer on the Muslim Separatists any right to go further, against the Indian facts of Indian history [vide *Poudyal v. Union of India*, A 1993 SC 1804 (paras 30, 51) CB]

Separate Homeland for All Muslims

Dawn of 23 March 2002

PROFESSOR ZIAUDDIN Ahmad has also written a front page article in the *Dawn* supplement dated 23 March 2002. He describes the events that led to the 1940 resolution where the demand for Pakistan was made at the Muslim League session in Lahore. Excerpts from his article are best reproduced so that the spirit and the flavour of what he has said are not missed.

> There is no denying the fact that the War of Independence of 1857, deprived the Muslims of their position, honour and prestige, for the British considered them as the potential danger to their rule. They were looked down upon with great suspicion and distrust and were victimised and punished on baseless excuses. The doors of employment for them in Government service were closed. Thus they were forced into humiliation and degradation.

> The position of Muslims was in a melting pot when fortunately Syed Ahmad Khan diagnosed it, felt the pulse of the nation and found a panacea for all their ills. With great determination and self confidence he took the first step to bring a political rapprochement between the ruler and the ruled. To revive knowledge and modern education Syed Ahmad Khan founded a Scientific Society with the main purpose of disseminating modern knowledge and scientific advancement. He also laid the foundation of Aligarh Muslim University in 1875, which awakened the Muslims and brought self-consciousness in them. His Tahzibul Akhlaq worked on the lines of the 18th century magazines 'The Spectator' and 'The Tatler,' to enlighten the Muslims with a view to accepting what was sound and useful in modern learning and science, and inculcate in them simplicity, honesty and virtues. He gathered a band of writers and thinkers like Hali, Shibli, Nazir Ahmed, Mohsin-ul-Mulk and Viqar-ul-Mulk who inspired the Muslims with an awakening to revive their lost glory and to look to the future with renewed hope.

Hector Bolitho, the famous biographer of Jinnah, has rightly remarked:

> The tragic circumstances of the Muslims at last bred the leader they needed. His name was Syed Ahmed Khan, the first Muslim in India who dared to speak of "Partition," the first to realise that, mutual adsorption being impossible, the Hindus and the Muslims must part.
>
> In 1867, when Hindus dominated Government offices and law courts, Syed Ahmed Khan felt convinced that it was now impossible for the Hindus and Muslims to progress as a single nation and for anyone to work

> for both of them simultaneously. With the passage of time the concept of independent destiny and separate political course which Syed Ahmed Khan had envisaged for the Muslims gained momentum. It led to the demand for separate electorates in the form of the Simla Deputation (1906) to the Viceroy, Lord Minto, who accepted separate electorates and laid the foundation of two nation theory and the historic Lahore Resolution of March 23, 1940, was its logical conclusion.
>
> After successful recognition of separate electorate by the Government, the Muslims felt the necessity of founding the All India Muslim League on December 30, 1906 for the protection and advancement of their political rights, their culture and religion and respectfully representing their needs and aspirations to the Government.

These ideas were expressed with clarity by Muhammad Ali, the most outstanding leader of the Khilafat Movement in his first issue of the *Comrade*, of January If), 1911. He said:

> We have no faith in the cry that India is united. The problems of India are almost international. We may not create today the patriotic fervour and the fine national frenzy of Japan with its 40 million of homogeneous people. But a concordant like that of Canada is not beyond the bounds of practicability. It may not be a love marriage born of romance and poetry, but a marriage of convenience honourably contracted and honourably maintained is not to be despised.

During Jinnah's participation in the Round Table Conference in London, he wrote a letter to the British Prime Minister in January 1931 in which he laid down a principle for the solution of the Hindu Muslim problem.

> The real problem before us is to give full power to Muslims in such provinces as those in which they are in a majority, whether large or small, and protection to them in such provinces as those in which they are in minority and in order to be absolutely fair to the Hindu community also precisely the same thing should be done with the Hindus. This principle may be reckoned as the basis for the evolution of the idea of Pakistan.

The Qaid-e-Azam, during his speech to the All India Muslim League in 1913, identified the causes which had created the fight between the Hindus and the Muslims. He said:

> There is but one question besides the question of cow killing and street music which had proved not only a thorny question but an obstacle which has kept the two communities hitherto apart. But the solution is not difficult. It required a true spirit of conciliation and give and take. The Mussulmans want proper, adequate and effective representation in the Council Chambers of the country and in district and municipal boards, a claim which no right minded Hindu disputes for a moment. But the Mussulmans further require that the representation in the various boards and Council Chambers should be secured for them by means of separate electorates. This question of separate electorates from top to bottom has been before the country ever since 1909 and rightly or wrongly the Mussulman community is absolutely determined for the present to insist upon separate electorates. To most of us, the question is no more open to further discussion or argument, as it has become a mandate of the community.

The Simla Deputation of 1906 gave some ray of hope to the Muslims for separate electorate but they received the greatest shock when King George V made an announcement on December 12, 1911 for the annulment of the partition of Bengal. The announcement at the Delhi Durbar led to a significant shift in Muslim thinking and policies. The confidence in the British Government that Muslims would be protected from Hindu aggressiveness was completely lost. The Muslim League objectives in favour of a form of government suitable to India were changed.

The international situation of the Muslim world also looked bleak with the Italian invasion of Tripolitania which was a Turkish province. The Anglo-Russian convention of 1906 reduced Iran to a mere dependency. Afghanistan lacked power to take advantage of the rivalry between Great Britain and Russia. Muslim North Africa had succumbed to European hegemony, the Turkish Empire, nicknamed the Sick Man of Europe came under western aggression ultimately was partitioned and dismembered into smaller units. All these political events greatly stirred the minds of the Muslims of the subcontinent. Britain's Prime Minister (1916-1922) Lloyd George emerged as an arch enemy of the Muslims.

In 1919, the *Khilafat* movement was started under the dynamic and inspiring leadership of Maulana Mohammad Ali Jauhar in order to awaken the Muslims and prepare the masses to boldly fight against the British highhandedness and injustice. MK Gandhi, a most shrewd brain, taking advantage of this situation put himself heart and soul in the movement. This Hindu-Muslim amity lasted for a very short period. The reason was that the Muslim awakening tended to overshadow the Hindu urge for *swaraj* under the protection of British bayonets, as Maulana Mohammad Ali once remarked.

In order to rebuild their community, the Hindus started the *Shuddhi* and *Sanghatan* movements which shattered the artificial bonds of unity. The Muslims started counter movements of *Tabligh* and *Tanzim*. The policy of Gandhiism betrayed the Muslims and exposed the hollowness of *Ahimsa* tactics.

Thereafter, prominent Muslim representatives of different opinions met in Delhi on 20 March 1927 at Mr MA Jinnah's invitation. After long deliberations they came to a final conclusion, the Delhi Muslim Proposals. The Congress agreed to these "proposals" but most Hindus did not agree and communal riots broke out all over India.

The Congress took up the challenge and convened an All Party Conference in December 1928 to draw up a constitution for India. It appointed a committee under the chairmanship of Pandit Motilal Nehru. Hence, the committee's report is known as the Nehru Report. It gave no special representation and safeguards to the Muslims. Therefore, it was totally rejected by the Muslims.

In order to unite the Muslims of all groups an All India Muslim Conference was held in Delhi in March 1929 to evolve a formula for Muslim rights and their safeguards. It came out with fourteen points which remained a pivot round which the whole Muslim political thought and activity revolved.

The idea of territorial consolidation is not new. As early as 1915, Choudhry Rahmat Ali addressing the *Bazm-l-Shibli* in the Islamia College said that the northern part of India consists of an overwhelming population of Muslims and it will be kept Muslim.

In 1917, the Khetri brothers Dr Abdul Jabbar Khetri and Prof Abdus Sattar Khetri, suggested a plan for the partition of India at the Stockholm Conference of the Socialist International. In April 1920, Muhammad Abdul Qadir Bilgrami published an open letter to Gandhi in the *Dhul-Qarnain* of Badayun advocating partition of India in Hindu and Muslim zones and even giving a list of districts. In 1923, Sardar Mohammad Gul Khan advocated the division of India between the Hindus and the Muslims before the Frontier Inquiry Committee.

In 1933, Choudhry Rahmat Ali, an erstwhile student at Cambridge issued a pamphlet entitled "Now or Never" in which the idea of a separate Muslim state in India called Pakistan was reiterated. In October 1938, at the Sind Muslim League Conference, Karachi, presided over by Quad-e-Azam Mohammad Ali Jinnah, Haji Abdullah Haroon, a veteran Muslim League leader. Advocating the partition of India moved a resolution urging that India be divided into two federations, one for Muslims and the other for non-Muslim groups.

The Government of India Act of 1919 which gave a very limited measure of reforms did not prove a success. Thereafter in 1927 the Simon Commission was appointed to review the working of the Act. The report of the Commission proved extremely disappointing to all concerned. The Congress started a civil disobedience movement. Maulana Mohammad Ali explained the Muslim attitude: We refuse to join Mr Gandhi because his movement is not a movement for the complete independence of India but for making the 70 million Mussulmans dependents of the Hindu Mahasabha.

Then the British Government convened a series of Round Table Conferences in 1930-3, which failed to solve the communal problem. After realising this, the British Prime Minister announced the Communal Award in August 1932. This was followed by the Government of India Act 1935 which established full provincial autonomy. The 1935 Act did not satisfy the Muslims. The Qaid-e-Azam therefore appointed a Special Committee in March 1939 to clarify the Muslim position in respect to the future constitution.

There seemed to be no other alternative left but to find a new and separate homeland. Therefore, at the Lahore session of the Muslim League on March 23 1940, the Qaid-e-Azam in his presidential address made an irrefutable case for a separate Muslim nation and for dividing India into Muslim and Hindu states. More than one lakh people attended this session and the resolution of 1940 became the *Magna Carta* of Muslim freedom.

Ethnic Cleansing by Pakistan

ETHNIC CLEANSING is an expression which earned an obnoxious connotation during the Serbo-Bosnian crisis of 1991-92. It was however the description of an exchange of population as prescribed in the Treaty of Lausanne of 1923 whereby the Greeks living in Turkey were to leave for resettlement in Greece and the Turks were to resettle permanently in Turkey. The Treaty was implemented faithfully as was the Convention of 1913 which set out the procedures of population transfer between Bulgaria and Turkey.

As detailed in the chapter titled Unfinished Agenda, the League leaders envisaged an exchange of population between the two new dominions resulting from Partition. The Muslims were to all gather in the new dominion of Pakistan whereas all non-Muslims were to remain. Congress leaders of the time paid no heed to the League demand and took the stand that India could not, in principle, consider losing its Muslim citizens.

Faithful to the League plan, the west Punjab began its programme of ethnic cleansing with determined single mindedness. They allowed their own citizens to take the law into their hands in anticipation of the Partition and permitted them to continue perpetrating loot, rape, murder and arson with the collective intent of frightening the non-Muslims to leave Pakistan. How they went about their mission is best gleaned through what Justice GD Khosla had to report to the then Government of India in 1948. His survey was subsequently published under the title Stern Reckoning. Quoted as follows are a few of the highlights from the survey and an extract from Ian Talbot's book.

By April 1946, Sir Feroze Khan Noon had evidently become impatient with the Congress leaders not agreeing to an exchange of population. In a speech made to the Muslim League legislators on the 9th of that month, he had threatened to re-enact the murderous orgies of Changez Khan and Halaqu Khan if the non-Muslims look up a refractory attitude. His was no idle threat. His followers were faithful to his call and put in practice the murderous orgies.

In Khushab Tehsil of the Punjab, the wealthy Batras of Girot and Mitha Tiwana resisted for two days. Ultimately, twenty three members of the family were arrested on false murder charges. They were safely evacuated only after expending huge sums of money to buy off their accusers. Bhagat Ram Chand, for example, handed over Rs 35,000 in hard cash. Mokam Singh a well known Sikh landowner of the Thai suffered a more nightmarish fate. He led the resistance to the Muslim attack on Roda village. When the defenders ammunition finally gave out, the settlement was overrun by a mob which beheaded him. His severed head was transfixed to a spear and paraded as a war trophy from village to village. News of the violence in the Khushab tehsil, spread as far as Nairobi, as stated by Ian Talbot in Khizr Tiwana, Curzon, Surrey, UK, 1996.

Let us now move to the Rawalpindi district with Justice Khosla:

Bewal was a village of mixed population, the Sikhs numbering about four hundred. On the morning of March 10, some of the Sikh residents tried to travel to Gujar Khan but the Muslim lorry driver refused to carry them on the ground that the Sub-Inspector of Police had forbidden the issue of lorry tickets to Sikhs. The same afternoon a large crowd of Muslims shouting "Ya Ali, Ya Ali," to the beating of drums, was seen approaching. The non-Muslim villagers entrenched themselves in two improvised shelters. At 11 pm the raiders set fire to a number of non-Muslim houses on the outskirts of the village. The siege of the village continued throughout the night, and, on the morning of March 11, fresh gangs of raiders arrived. The assault on the non-Muslim sanctuaries was now opened. Houses around the Gurdwara, where many of the Sikh residents had taken shelter, were set on fire. The fire spread to the Gurdwara and those inside were almost all burnt alive. The house of a retired Extra Assistant Commissioner, in which the rest of the non-Muslims had collected, was also attacked in a similar manner. Very few of the four hundred Sikh residents escaped alive.

Many women and girls saved their honour by self-immolation. They collected their beddings and cots in a heap and when the heap caught fire they jumped on to it raising cries of Sat Sri Akal. The raiders behaved in a most cruel manner and subjected the few men whom they captured to torture. The eyes of Mukand Singh, one of the residents, were removed from their sockets and he was dragged by the legs till he died.

On the morning of March 10, swarms of armed raiders from the neighbouring villages began to collect in front of Doberan, which had a population of seventeen hundred of whom a very large majority were Sikhs.. The non-Muslim residents sought shelter in the local Gurdwara. The raiders began to loot the houses thus deserted and set fire to them. The Sikhs had a few firearms and fought the raiders from the Gurdwara. They, however, suffered heavily and soon ran out of ammunition. The raiders asked them to surrender their arms and promised not to molest them. About three hundred of them came out and they were placed in the house of one Barkat Singh. During the night the roof was ripped open, kerosene was poured in, and those inside were burnt alive. In the morning the doors of the Gurdwara were broken open. The remaining Sikhs dashed out sword in hand and died fighting the raiders. Very few escaped from this hideous massacre. The total loss of life in this village is estimated at 506.

In Qazian, a village five miles from Gujar Khan, the atmosphere on the morning oj March 7 was tense. Qazi Ghulam Hussain, a retired Government official, assured the Sikh residents that there was no cause Jor alarm and that they were perfectly safe in his village. On the moming of March 9, a large crowd of Muslims began to assemble near the village abadi on the pretence of holding a kabaddi match. The Muslims advanced with the beat of drums and began setting fire to the Sikh houses and Gurdwara. Shots were fired at the raiders and they retreated. On the following morning they came back, reinforced in larger numbers.

Qazi Ghulam Hussain asked the Sikhs to come to his house for the night with their valuables. A number of Sikhs accepted this invitation and went there with their women and children. At 4 pm the raiders appeared in front of Qazi Ghulam Hussain's house and the Qazi then asked his guests to surrender their arms and leave his house. When the unarmed Sikhs emerged from the house they were set upon by the raiders and murdered. Three young girls were raped in public. Sant Singh, a Sikh resident had on the previous day killed one of the Muslim raiders and had then hidden himself. He was sent for by Qazi Ghulam Hussain and while he was talking to him a rope was flung round his neck and he was dragged to a fire wood stall where he and his son were hacked to bits and then burnt. The survivors were evacuated to Gujar Khan by military lorries on the night of the 11th.

Nara village is situated in a hilly tract. It had a majority of Sikhs but the neighbouring villagers were all predominantly Muslim. At about 4 pm on March 9. Muslim mobs were seen approaching the village and. late at night the village was attacked and the outlying houses were set on fire. One of the residents, Makhan Singh and his wife and daughter were burnt alive in their house. The looting and burning continued on the following day. Some of the raiders had firearms and they appeared to be ex-military men. On March 11 the number of raiders swelled to several thousands and the village was encircled. As the ring narrowed the Sikh residents offered stubborn resistance. The raiders seized a number of women and children and threw them into the blaze of a burning house. A few women committed suicide by jumping into a well. Over a hundred men were killed, about fifty were forcibly converted to Islam. The survivors were evacuated to Gujar Khan.

In Sialkot district: conversion to Islam was frequently offered as the price of safety, and if the victims exhibited any reluctance or religious scruples they were subjected to duress and torture. The hair of Sikhs was' cut off, their beards were trimmed and beef was cooked and forced down their throats. Some of them were circumcised. Young women and girls were molested and carried away. Reason and decency were completely banished by fanatical zeal and young innocent girls were raped in public. In one village the relations of a girl were made to stand around in a ring while she was raped by several men in succession.

Moving to Sheikhupura, not far from the birthplace of Guru Nanak, here is a heart rending eye witness account of the Civil Surgeon. 'Whosoever tried to run away fell a victim to the shots of the Baluchis and the policemen. Having thus cleared away all the living population the looters began to ransack the houses under the very nose of the policemen. At about 10 o'clock, trench-mortar fire was heard in Guru Nanak Pura locality. In all we heard about ten mortar shots. Since the firing came nearer and nearer to the hospital and the people had been killed under our very noses, we hid ourselves in the dark room attached to the X-Ray Department of the hospital. It proved to be the safest place. While hiding there in the dark room we heard woeful cries of Hindu and Sikh children as they were done to death by the Muslim mob. The cry of one child was particularly heart-rending. At about 2 pm we heard the cry, "Do not cut my throat. Do not cut my throat. You have already killed my parents. Take me with you". He was killed in the hospital verandah about twenty paces from us.'

These crimes overtook the cruelty of even Changez Khan and Halaqu Khan, the heroes of Sir Feroze Khan Noon.

Justice Khosla's report ends by summing up: that League ideology and the line of conduct pursued by it were mainly and directly responsible for the horrible drama, narrated in these pages, is clearly demonstrated by the inexorable logic of chronology. The speeches delivered at the Convention of the Muslim League legislators in April 1946, were an open incitement to violence. On July 29, the Direct Action resolution frankly abjured peaceful and constitutional methods and, on August 16, the campaign of violence was opened at Calcutta under the command and guidance of Mr Suhrawardy. In October came the tragedy oj Noakhali and Tippera. Almost immediately afterwards retaliation followed in Bihar. Then, for some months there was a lull while a major operation in the North-west was being planned. With the riots of March 1947 began the genocide of the non-Muslims. These disturbances were confined to the Muslim majority areas only and the victims were almost invariably Hindus and Sikhs.

There was emigration during 1947 and early 1948 from East Punjab to Pakistani Punjab. To a significant extent, therefore, the two portions of the Punjab did achieve an exchange of population. There were only some scattered emigrations from other parts of the country, whether Gujarat, DP, Bihar or Bengal; the number was small. This in no way could represent anything like an exchange of population, not to speak of ethnic cleansing.

Why No Hindu-Christian Riots?

THE KILLINGS in Godhra and elsewhere in Gujarat are a sharp reminder that riots are not infrequent occurrences in our country. For over a century, not many years have passed when there has been no riot somewhere or the other in the subcontinent. Before that, there might have been occurrences but no records are available in the English language. The first time, the provocation was cow slaughter Bombay and Azamgarh.

Christians also eat beef but never has one come across a Christian riot or a Hindu-Christian collective clash. Christians have also ruled India and, in fact, more comprehensively than any Muslim potentate. They slowly but surely carried away the economic surpluses of the Indian economy. Muslim rulers generally did not, unless one recalls the plunder by Mahmud Ghazni, Nadir Shah and a few others.

Christian proselytizers have been more professional and organized than their Muslim counterparts. The oppression, especially by the Portuguese missionaries, are comparable to the atrocities by Islamic bigots. It is not that temple desecrations were a Muslim monopoly. Christian iconoclasts in their early years in India were also ruthless. Our problems in the northeast would have been fewer but for the brainwashing of the tribals with regard to their equation with New Delhi. Yet there is neither any record nor memory of a Christian riot.

Some apologists argue that there is really no difference, except that Muslims are much more in numbers and therefore a larger minority than the Christians and the potential therefore for a clash with the latter is less. This is true but experience shows absolutely no Christian rioting and not less rioting. Second, a communal riot does not take place across the country on a national scale. It usually takes place in a city, town or a district, and occasionally spreads to other parts of the same or even a neighbouring state. For example, the Bhagalpur riots in Bihar or the many occurrences in Bhiwandi or, for that matter, the recent happenings in Gujarat, none of them spread to other regions.

Essentially, a riot is a local clash and, to begin with, is usually confined to a particular locality. There are more Christians in Tamil Nadu than there are Muslims. In Kerala, there are Christians and Muslims in large numbers with the former exceeding the latter but one has never heard of Christians being involved in a physical clash. Tamil Nadu had its trouble spots like Coimbatore in the west and Chennai in the east, but that did not involve Christians. Kerala has a longer and larger tradition. The Moplah riots of 1920 was a holocaust whereas there have been several recent episodes including in the commercial streets of Mattancherry in Kochi.

This is not to lay blame on any religion or community. In any case, Christianity and Islam are both religions of the Book and most of their prophets are common, beginning with Abraham. The comparison is to underline the need for an investigation into the causes of riots by sociologists. This science of society has regrettably overlooked its duty towards innocent lives that suffer every time there is a riot. Even more than duty sociologists owe an obligation to humanity. The reason is simple, the lives that are lost and the suffering that takes place is not by the rioters but by common people.

The criminals who set on fire the railway coach in Godhra have yet to be punished, but 58 innocents including women and children, lost their lives by being burnt alive. Thereafter, most of those who indulged in arson and killing on the streets of Ahmedabad or elsewhere, are unlikely to be caught whereas, people unconcerned with Godhra, terrorism or politics, have suffered untold misery. Sociologists may have conducted research, but they have not come up with any clue as to how rioting can be prevented, or rather pre-empted. Most of the time, suggestions are of an administrative or police nature, like the creation of a rapid action force.

There are more Christians in Gujarat than is popularly

perceived. Fifteen percent of the state's population is Adivasi. They are present in great numbers across the southern and eastern districts like Baroda, Surat, Valsad, Panchmahal and Sabarkantha. Not to forget the tiny district of the Dangs which was in limelight a few years ago for raging tensions over proselytizing activity. Yet, to this day there has been no riot and neither has a Christian been killed, nor has a Hindu lost his life, as a result of this or any other tension. Surely, it is more than sufficient food for thought for the sociologists to conduct research. In the absence of any study and suggested solutions, myths are likely to flourish and rumours probably would provide causes for flare ups in the future.

Hindu nationalist scholars believe that riots are an expression of a deep rooted frustration suffered by the Muslims who are in a minority in a country, or rather in a society, where the writ of the *sharia* does not run. Not to say that this complex is in the mind of the miscreant who lights the flame of a riot. He only expresses violence that is bugging the bosoms of his fellow men. It is not that he is aware that if he were a *Momin* or a devout Muslim, it would be his duty to get *kafirs* or non-believers to surrender to the will of Allah the Merciful. If he cannot do it by persuasion, he has to resort to *jihad* or war for the sake of God and religion.

If, however, *jihad* is not possible or the prospects of its success hopeless, the *Momin* should resort to *hijrat*. The Holy Prophet himself set the first example when he migrated or performed *hijrat* from Mecca to Medina. That was the only way he could save Islam from being virtually stillborn. When the British government proved unbending in its policy towards retaining the caliph of all Sunni Islam on the throne of Turkey, Indian Muslims became despondent. In 1920, several hundred thousand Indian Muslims undertook *hijrat* to Afghanistan which was a *Darul Islam.* About 20,000 of them entered the Afghan country and settled there.

Mahatma Gandhi also recommended *hijrat* to Sindh for Hindus when they were oppressed by riots in Sukkur and Shikarpur. He justified his advice by saying: '*Planned hijrat requires courage and forethought. The second book of the Old Testament is known as Exodus. It is an account of the planned flight of the Israelites.* This is quoted from Volume 71 of the *Collected Works of Mahatma Gandhi*, Publications Division, Government of India.

In sharp contrast to the nationalist perception, secularists generally believe that communal riots are provoked by Hindu militants like those who insist on building a Ram Mandir at Ayodhya. There are two sharply opposed opinions. The time is now more than overdue for sociologists to undertake the required study and to establish *facts*. So that opinions based on ideological predilections can be buried. The hope is that the resulting analysis will provide the basis for pursuing appropriate measures to pre-empt communal riots.

Conclusion

MA Jinnah and seven other leaders of the Muslim League through 1946 and early 1947 repeatedly demanded that ideally, *all* Muslims should migrate from the boundaries of Hindustan to what was going to be Pakistan. Similarly, all Hindus and Sikhs should relocate from the boundaries of Pakistan to Hindustan. Those who could not migrate would stay back as a minority and serve the function of reciprocal hostages. If Muslims were mistreated in Hindustan, Pakistan would retaliate against the Hindus living there. So said Jinnah, whose exclusive idea *retaliation* was.

Dr Rajendra Prasad, India's *Rashtrapati* for the first two terms of the republic, wrote a book *India Divided*. Therein he proposed that the two minorities would live as aliens on the strength of visas issued by the respective governments. Jinnah readily agreed with this formulation. These proposals could not go forward because of the stubborn resistance of MK Gandhi.

When Syamaprasad Mookerjee saw that refugees in large numbers were arriving in India, accompanied by Rajkumari

Amrit Kaur, he went to see Gandhi in order to appeal to him to accept the Jinnah thesis of a population exchange. The great man instantly rejected the appeal and added that Partition was a 'territorial' division and had 'nothing to do with religion'. This visit of Syamaprasad and the Rajkumari is part of a parliamentary speech. No matter what was said and discussed before Partition, it was scuttled after Partition by free India's independent government which chose a future of strife with eyes open.

Letters

I

GANDHIJI TO RAJAJI
September 9, 1944

It was a test of my patience. I am amazed at my own patience. However, it was a friendly talk.

"His (Jinnah's) contempt for your Formula (Rajaji Formula) and his contempt for you is staggering. You rose in my estimation that you could have talked to him for all those hours and that you should have taken the trouble to draw up that formula. He says you have accepted his demand and so should I."

I said, "I endorse Rajaji's Formula and you can call it Pakistan if you like." He talked of the Lahore Resolution. I said, "I have not studied it and I do not want to talk about it. Let us talk about Rajaji's Formula and you can point out any flaws that you find there."

In the middle of the talk he came back to the old

ghost: "I thought you had come here as a Hindu, as a representative of the Hindu Congress."

I said, "No, I have come here neither as a Hindu nor as a representative of the Congress. I have come here as an individual. You can talk to me as an individual or as the President of the League, whichever way you prefer. If you had agreed with Rajaji and accepted his Formula, you and he would have gone before your respective organizations and pleaded with them to accept it. That is why Rajaji came to you. You would then have placed it before other parties, too, in the same way. Now you and I have to do it."

He said that he was the President of the League. Where was the basis for a talk if I was there representing nobody except myself? Who was to deliver the goods? I was the same man as he had found me in 1939. There was no change in me. I almost felt like saying, "Yes, I am the same man and since you think it is no use talking to me, I will go away." But I resisted the temptation. I told him, "Is it not worth your while to convert an individual? I am the same man no doubt. You can change my views if you can and I will support you whole-heartedly."

"Yes, I know, if I can convert you, you will be my Ali," he said. He said, "I should concede Pakistan and he would go the whole length with me. He would go to jail, he would even face bullets." I said, "I will stand by your side to face them." "You may not," he said. "Try me," I replied.

We came back to the Formula. He wants Pakistan now, not after Independence. "We will have Independence for Pakistan and Hindustan," he said.

"We should come to an agreement and then go to the Government and ask them to accept it, force them to accept our solution." I said, "I could never be a party to that. I could never ask the Britishers to impose partition on India."

"If you all want to separate, I can't stop you. I have not got the power to compel you and I would not use it if I had." He said, "The Muslims want Pakistan. The League represents the Muslims and it wants separation."

I said, "I agree the League is the most powerful Muslim organization. I might even concede that you as its President, represent the Muslims of India, but that does not mean that all Muslims want Pakistan. Put it to the vote of all the inhabitants of the area and see."

He said, "Why should you ask non-Muslims?"

I said, "You cannot possibly deprive a section of the population of its vote. You must carry them with you, and if you are in the majority why should you be afraid?" I told him of what Kiron Shankar Roy had said to me: "If the worst comes to the worst, we in Bengal will all go in Pakistan, but for goodness sake do not partition Bengal. Do not vivisect it."

"If you are in majority," I said, "you will have your choice."

"I know it is a bad thing for you, but if you want it all the same you will have it. But that will be an adjustment between you and mc. It cannot occur while the Britishers are here."

He began to cross-examine me on the various clauses of the Formula. I said to him, "If you want clarification of those things, is it not better to have it from the author of the Formula?" He did not want that.

I said, "What is the use of your cross-examining me?"

He recollected himself. "Oh no! I am not cross-examining you." And then added: "I have been a lawyer all my life and my manner may have suggested that I was cross-examining you."

I asked him to reduce to writing his objections to the Formula. He was disinclined. "Must 1 do so?" he asked.

"Yes, I would like you to." He agreed.

In the end he said, "I would like to come to an agreement with you."

I answered, "You remember that I have said that we should meet not to separate till we had come to an agreement.

He said, "Yes,"

I suggested, "Should we put that also in our statement?"

He said, "No, better not. Nevertheless that will be the understanding between us and the cordiality and friendliness of our talk will be reflected in our public utterances too."

II

LETTER FROM M A JINNAH

September 10, 1944

Dear Mr Gandhi,

With reference to our talk yesterday, September 9th, I understood from you that you had come to discuss the Hindu-Muslim settlement with me in your individual capacity, and not in any representative character or capacity on behalf of the Hindus or the Congress, nor had you any authority to do so. I naturally pointed out to you that there must be someone on the other side with authority holding a representative status with whom I can negotiate and, if possible, come to a settlement of the Hindu-Muslim question, and that, for the position you had adopted there was no precedent, and that, this raises great difficulties in my way. As you know, I can only speak on behalf of Muslim India and the All-India Muslim League, as the President of the organization which I represent, and as such I am subject to and governed by its constitution, rules and regulations. I think you realize and will admit that the settlement of the Hindu-Muslim question is the foremost and the major hurdle, and unless the representatives of these two nations put their heads together, how is one to make any headway with it?

Nevertheless, I explained to you the Lahore Resolution of March 1940, and tried to persuade you to accept the basic and fundamental principles embodied in that resolution, but you not only refused to consider it but emphasised your opposition to the basic position indicated in the resolution, and remarked that there was "an ocean between you and me", and when I asked you what is then the alternative you suggest, you put forward a formula of Mr Rajagopalachari, approved of by you. We discussed it, and as the various matters were vague and nebulous, and some required clarification, I wanted to have a clear idea of what it really meant, and what were its implications, and asked you for explanation and clarification regarding the proposals embodied in that Formula. After some discussion, you requested me to formulate in writing my points that I thought required or called for explanation and clarification, and to communicate with you and that you would reply in writing before our next meeting on Monday, September 11th, at 5.30 pm I am, therefore, submitting to you the following points which required clarification:

1. With regard to the preamble: in what capacity will you be a consenting party if any agreement is reached between you and me?
2. Clause I: With regard to "the constitution for

free India" referred to in this clause, I would like to know first, what constitution do you refer to, who will frame it, and when will it come into being?

Next, it is stated in the Formula that 'the Muslim League endorses the Indian demand for independence.' Does it mean the Congress demand for Independence as formulated in the August Resolution of 1942 by the All-India Congress Committee in Bombay or, if not, what is the significance of this term, for you know the Muslim League has made it clear not only by its resolutions but also by its creed, which is embodied in its constitution, that we stand for the freedom and independence of the whole of this subcontinent, and that applies to Pakistan and Hindustan.

Next, it is stated that the Muslim League 'will cooperate with the Congress in the formulation of a Provisional Interim Government for the transitional Period'. I would like to know the basis or the lines on which such a Government is to be set up or constituted. If you have a complete and definite scheme, please let me have it.

3. Clause 2: Who will appoint the Commission referred to in this clause and who will give effect to their findings? What is the meaning of 'absolute majority' referred to in it? Will the contemplated plebiscite be taken district-wise, or, if not, on what basis? Who will determine and decide whether such a plebiscite should be based on adult franchise or other practicable franchise?

Who will give effect to the decision or verdict of the above mentioned plebiscite? Would only the districts on the border which are taken out from the boundaries of the present provinces by delimitation be entitled to choose to join either State or also those outside the present boundaries would have the right to choose to join either State?

4. Clause 3: Who are meant by 'all parties' in this clause?
5. Clause 4: I would like to know between whom and through what machinery and agency will the 'mutual agreements' referred to in this clause be entered into? What is meant by 'safeguarding defence and commerce, communications and for other essential purposes'? Safeguarding against whom?
6. Clause 6: 'These terms shall be binding, only in case of transfer by Britain of full power and responsibility for the Government of India.' I would like to know to whom is this power to be transferred, through what machinery and agency, and when?

These are some of the important points that occur to me for the moment, which require explanation and clarification, and hope that you will let me have full details with regard to the various points that I have raised, in order that I may be better able to understand and judge your proposals before I can deal with them satisfactorily.

Your sincerely,
JINNAH

III

LETTER TO M A JINNAH

September 11, 1944

Dear Qaid-E-Azam,

I received your letter yesterday at 3.30 pm I was in the midst of appointments. I hasten to reply at the earliest opportunity.

I have said in my letter to you, it is implied in the Rajaji Formula and I have stated publicly that I have approached you as an individual. My life mission has been Hindu-Muslim unity, which I want for its own sake, but which is not to be achieved without the foreign ruling power being ousted. Hence, the first condition of the exercise of the right of self-determination is achieving Independence by the joint action of all the parties and groups comprising India. If such a joint action is unfortunately impossible, then too I must fight with the assistance of such elements as can be brought together. I am glad, therefore, that you did not break off our talks when I refused to assume or accept a representative capacity. Of course I am pledged to use all the influence I may have with the Congress to ratify my agreement with you. May I remind you that the Rajaji Formula was designed in the first instance for your acceptance, and submission thereafter to the League?

It is true that I said an ocean separated you and me in outlook. But that had no reference to the Lahore Resolution of the League. The Lahore Resolution is indefinite. Rajaji has taken from it the substance and given it a shape.

Now for the points raised by you:

1. I have already answered this in the foregoing.
2. The constitution will be framed by the Provisional Government contemplated in the Formula or an authority specially set up by it after the British power is withdrawn. The Independence contemplated is of the whole of India as it stands. The basis for the formation of Provisional Interim Government will have to be agreed to between the League and the Congress.
3. The Commission will be appointed by the Provisional Government. "Absolute majority" means a clear majority over non-Muslim elements as in Sind, Baluchistan or the Frontier Province. The form of plebiscite and the franchise must be a matter for discussion.
4. "All parties" means, the parties interested.
5. "Mutual agreement" means agreement between contracting parties. "Safeguarding defence, etc.,"

means for me a central or joint board of control Safeguarding means safeguarding against all who may put the common interests in jeopardy.

6. The power is to be transferred to the nation, that is, to the Provisional Government. The Formula contemplates peaceful transfer by the British Government. So far as I am concerned I would like the transfer to take place as early as possible.

Yours sincerely,
M K GANDHI

IV

LETTER FROM M A JINNAH

September 11, 1944

Dear Mr Gandhi,

I received your letter of September 11 at 5 pm today. I note that you have approached me as an individual, and I have already expressed my views about it. Please do not take it that I acquiesce in the position that you have adopted, for which there is no precedent. Nevertheless, I proceeded to discuss matters with you naturally because I am anxious to convert you to my point of view, if possible. I urged you that the only solution of India's problem is to accept the division of India as Pakistan and Hindustan, as briefly laid down in the Lahore Resolution of March 1940, and proceed to settle the details forth with. You say the Lahore Resolution is indefinite. You never asked me for any clarification or explanation of the terms of the.

Resolution, but you really indicated your emphatic opposition to the very basis and the fundamental principles embodied in it. I would, therefore, like to know in what way or respect the Lahore Resolution is indefinite. I cannot agree that Rajaji has taken from it its substance and given it shape. On the contrary, he has not only put it out of shape but mutilated it, as I explained in my speech which I delivered at the meeting of the Council of the All-India Muslim League at Lahore on the 30th of July, 1944.

2. You say the "first condition of the exercise of the right of self-determination is achieving independence by the joint action of all the parties and groups composing India. If such joint action is unfortunately impossible, then, too, I must fight with the assistance of such elements as can be brought together". This in my opinion is, as I have repeatedly said, putting the cart before the horse, and is opposed to the policy and declarations of the All-India Muslim League and you are only holding on firmly to the August Resolution of 1942. In order to achieve the freedom and independence of the peoples of India, it is essential, in the first instance, that there should be a Hindu-Muslim settlement.

Of course I am thankful to you when you say that you are pledged to use all the influence that you have with the Congress to ratify your agreement with me, but that is not enough in my judgement, although it will be a very valuable help to me. I once more ask you to please let me know what is your concept of the basis for the formation of a Provisional Interim Government. No doubt it will be subject to agreement between the League and the Congress, but I think in fairness you should at least give me some rough idea of the lines of your conception, for you must have thought it out by now, and I would like to know what are your proposals or scheme for the formation of a provisional interim Government, which can give me some clear picture to understand it.

3. You have omitted to answer my question as to who will give effect to the findings of the Commission, and also it is not clear to me what you mean by absolute majority, when you say it means 'a clear majority over non-Muslim elements as in Sind, Baluchistan or the Frontier Province'. You have not even replied to my question as to who will decide the form of the plebiscite and the franchise contemplated by the Formula.

4. The answer does not carry any clear idea when you say 'all parties means parties interested'.

5. You say mutual agreement means agreement between the contracting parties,who are the contracting parties once a Provisional Interim Government is established of your conception? Who will appoint the Central or Joint Board of Control, which will safeguard defence, etc., and on what principle, through what machinery and agency, and subject to whose control and orders will such a central or Joint Board be?

6. You say 'the power is to be transferred to the nation, that is, to the Provisional Government.' That is all the greater reason why I would like to know full details of the Provisional Government as contemplated by you and of your conception.

Your sincerely,
JINNAH

V

GANDHIJI TO RAJAJI

Talk with M A Jinnah

September 12, 1944

GANDHIJI: He drew a very alluring picture of the Government of Pakistan. It would be a perfect democracy. I asked him if he had not told me that democracy did not suit Indian conditions. He did not remember it. He asked me to tell him what he had said. So I told him all that and said that I might have misunderstood him. In that case he should correct me. But when I repeated in detail what he had said, he could not say no.

He said, "Yes, he had said that, but that was with regard to imposed democracy." Then he said, "Do you think it is a question of religious minority with us?"

I said, "Yes. If not, he should tell me what it was."

He harangued, "I won't repeat all that here."

I asked him, "What would happen to the other minorities in Pakistan: Sikhs, Christians, Depressed Classes, etc."

He said that they would be part of Pakistan. I asked him if he meant joint electorates. He knew I was coming to it.

He said, "Yes, he would like them to be a part of the whole. He would explain the advantages of joint electorates, but if they wanted separate electorates they would have it. Sikhs would have Gurumukhi if they wanted and the Pakistan Government would give them financial aid."

I asked, "What about Jats?"

At first he pooh-poohed the idea. Then he said, "If they want it, they will also have it. They will have separate existence if they want it."

I said, "What about Christians? They also want some place where they are in a majority and where they can rule, as for instance in Travancore?"

He said that was a problem for the Hindus.

I said, "Supposing Travancore was in Pakistan?

He said that he would give it to them. He cited the instance of Newfoundland.

The rest of the talk was nothing. I am to continue exploring his mind.

VI

LETTER TO M A JINNAH

September 14, 1944

Dear Qaid-E-Azam,

I have your letter of the 13th instant. I understood from our talks that you were in no hurry for my answer. I was, therefore, taking the matter in a leisurely fashion, even hoping that as our talks proceeded and as cordiality increased, mutual clarification would come of itself and that we would only have to record our final agreement. But I understand and appreciate the other viewpoint. We should take nothing for granted. I should clarify your difficulties in understanding the Rajaji Formula and you should do likewise regarding yours, i.e., the Muslim League Lahore Resolution of 1940.

With reference to the Lahore Resolution, as agreed between us I shall deal with it in a separate letter. Perhaps at the end of our discussion, we shall discover that Rajaji not only has not put the Lahore Resolution out of shape and mutilated it but has given it substance and form. Indeed, in view of your dislike of the Rajaji Formula, I have, at any rate for the moment, put it out of my mind and I am concentrating on the Lahore Resolution in the hope of finding a ground for mutual agreement. So much, for the first paragraph of your letter.

As to the second, I do hold that unless we oust the third party we shall not be able to live at peace with one another. That does not mean that I may not make an effort to find ways and means of establishing a living peace between us. You ask for my conception of the basis for a provisional interim government. I would have told you if I had any scheme in mind. I imagine that if we two can agree it would be for us to consult the other parties. I can say this, that any provisional government to inspire confidence at the present moment must represent all parties. When that moment arrives, I shall have been replaced by some authoritative person, though you will have me always at your beck and call when you have converted me or you, by mutual conversion, we have become one functioning through two bodies.

As to the third point, the provisional government, being the appointing authority, will give effect to the findings of the Commission. This, I thought, was implied in my previous answer. Rajaji tells me that 'absolute majority' is used in his Formula in the same sense as it is used in ordinary legal parlance wherever more than two groups are dealt with. I cling to my own answer. But you will perhaps suggest a third meaning and persuade me to accept it.

The form of the plebiscite and franchise must be left to be decided by the provisional interim government unless we decide it now. I should say it should be by adult suffrage of all the inhabitants of the Pakistan area.

to the fourth, 'all parties' means you and I and everyone else holding views on the question at issue will and should seek by peaceful persuasion to influence public opinion as is done where democracy functions wholly or in part.

As to the fifth, supposing that the result of the plebiscite is in favour of partition, the provisional government will draft the treaty and agreements as regards the administration of matters of common interest, but the same has to be confirmed and ratified by the governments of the two States. The machinery required for the settlement and administration of matters of common interest will, in the first instance, be planned by the interim government, but subsequently will be matter for settlement between the two governments acting through the agencies appointed by each for that purpose.

As to the sixth, I hope the foregoing makes superfluous any further reply.

Yours sincerely,
M K GANDHI

VII

LETTER FROM M A JINNAH
September 14, 1944

Dear Mr Gandhi,

I received your letter of September 14 at 4.45 p.m. today in reply to my letter of September 11(and not of September 13 as you state, which seems to be a mistake) and I thank you for it.

1. Please let me have as soon as you can your promised letter indicating in what way or respect the Lahore Resolution is 'indefinite'.
2. With regard to the provision in the Gandhi-Rajaji Formula that 'the Muslim League endorses the Indian demand for Independence', I asked you in my letter dated September 10, 'does it mean the Congress demand for independence, as formulated in the August 1942 Resolution by

> the All-India Congress Committee in Bombay or, if not, what is the significance of this term?', to which you replied by your letter of September 11, 'The Independence contemplated is of the whole of India as it stands.' Hence I again ask, does it mean on the basis of a United India? I find that you have not clarified the point satisfactorily.

As regards the next part of the clause, the Formula proceeds to lay down that 'the Muslim League will cooperate with the Congress in the formation of the Provisional Interim Government for the transitional period'. I requested you by my letter of September 10 to let me know 'the basis or the lines on which such a Government is to be set up or constituted. If you have a complete and definite scheme, please let me have it' to which you replied by your letter of September 11 under reply that 'the basis for the formation of the Provisional Interim Government will have to be agreed to between the League and the Congress.' But that is not meeting my request for clarification, or giving me at least the outlines of such a Government. And that is what I have been asking for.

I hope that you do appreciate my point when I am requesting you to let me have rough outlines of the proposed Provisional Interim Government according to the Formula, so that I may have some idea. Of course, I can quite understand that such a Provisional Interim Government will represent all the parties and would be of a character that will inspire confidence at the present moment of all the parties. I can quite understand that when the moment arrives, certain things may follow but before we can deal with this Formula in a satisfactory manner, I repeat again that as it is your Formula, you should give me a rough idea of the Provisional Interim Government that will represent all the parties and would be of a character that will inspire confidence at the present moment of all the parties.

I can quite understand that when the moment arrives, certain things may follow but before we can deal with this Formula in a satisfactory manner. I repeat again that as it is your Formula, you should give me a rough idea of the provisional Interim Government that you contemplate. What I would like to know would be, what will be the powers of such a Provisional Interim Government, how will it be formed, to whom will it be responsible, and what will be its composition, etc. You, being the sponsor of this Gandhi- Rajaji Formula, should give me some rough idea and picture of it, so that I may understand what this part of the Formula means.

In your letter of September 14 in reply to my letter of Septemer 11, you inform me that you would have told me if you had any scheme in mind. I imagine that if we two can agree it would be for us to consult the 'other parties', but that is just the point. Unless I have some outlines or scheme, however rough, from you what are we to discuss in order to reach any agreement?

As regards the other matters which you have further explained, 1 have noted the explanation, and I do not think I need press you further, although some of them are not quite satisfactory.

Yours sincerely,
JINNAH

VIII

LETTER TO M A JINNAH

September 15, 1944

Dear Qaid-e-Azam,

This is in terms of our talks of Wednesday the 13th instant.

For the moment I have shunted the Rajaji Formula and with your assistance am applying my mind very seriously to the famous Lahore Resolution of the Muslim League.

You must admit that the Resolution itself makes no reference to the two nation theory. In the course of our discussions, you have passionately pleaded that India contains two nations, i.e., Hindus and Muslims, and that the latter have their homelands in India as the former have theirs. The more our argument progresses, the more alarming your picture appears to me. It would be alluring if it was true. But my fear is growing that it is wholly unreal. I find no parallel in history for a body of converts and their descendants claiming to be a nation apart from the parent stock. If India was one nation before the advent of Islam, it must remain one in spite of the change of faith of a very large body of her children.

You do not claim to be a separate nation by right of conquest, but by reason of acceptance of Islam. Will the two nations become one if the whole of India accepted Islam? Will Bengalis, Oriyas, Andhras, Tamilians, Maharashtrians, Gujaratis, etc., cease to have their special characteristics if all of them become converts to Islam? These have all become one politically because they are subject to one foreign control. They are trying today to throw off that subjection.

You seem to have introduced a new test of nationhood. If I accept it, I would have to subscribe to many more claims and face an insoluble problem. The only real, though awful, test of our nationhood arises out of our common political subjection. If you and I throw off this subjection by our combined effort, we shall be born a politically free nation out of our travails. If by then we have not learnt to prize our freedom, we may quarrel among ourselves and, for want of a common master holding us together in his iron grip, seek to split up into small groups or nationalities. There will be nothing to prevent us from descending to that level and we shall not have to go in search of a master. There are many claimants to the throne that never remains vacant.

With this background, I shall present you with my difficulty in accepting your Resolution.

1. Pakistan is not in the Resolution. Does it bear the original meaning Punjab, Afghanistan, Kashmir, Sind and Baluchistan, out of which the name was mnemonically formed? If not what is it?
2. Is the goal of Pakistan pan-Islam?
3. What is it that distinguishes an Indian Muslim from every other Indian, if not his religion? Is he different from a Turk or an Arab?
4. What is the connotation of the word "Muslims" in the Resolution under discussion? Does it mean the Muslims of India of geography or of the Pakistan to be?
5. Is the Resolution addressed to the Muslims by way of education, or to the inhabitants of the whole of India by way of appeal, 01, to the foreign ruler as an ultimatum?
6. Are the constituents in the two Zones to constitute "Independent States", with an undefined number in each zone?
7. Is the demarcation to take place during the pendency of British Rule?
8. If the answer to the last question is in the affirmative, the proposal must be accepted first by Britain and then imposed upon India, not evolved from within by the free will of the people of India.
9. Have you examined the position and satisfied yourself that these 'Independent States' will be materially and otherwise benefited by being split up into fragments?
10. Please satisfy me that these Independent Sovereign States will not become a collection of

poor States, a menace to themselves and to the rest of India.

11. Pray show me by facts and figures or otherwise how the independence and welfare of India as a whole can be brought about by the acceptance of the Resolution?
12. How are the Muslims under the Princes to be disposed as a result of this scheme?
13. What is your definition of 'minorities'?
14. Will you please define the 'adequate, effective and mandatory safeguards' for minorities referred to in the second part of the Resolution?
15. Do you not see that the Lahore Resolution contains only a bare statement of the objective and does not give any idea as to the means to be adopted for the execution of the idea and the concrete corollaries thereof? For instance:
    (a) Are the people in the regions falling under the plan to have any voice in the matter of separation and, if so, how is it to be ascertained?
    (b) What is the provision for defence and similar matters of common concern contemplated in the Lahore Resolution?
    (c) There are many groups of Muslims who have continuously expressed dissent about the policy of the League. While I am prepared to accept the prepondering influence and position of the League and have approached you for that very reason, is it not our joint duty to remove their doubts and carry them with us by making them feel that they and

their supporters have not been practically disfranchised?

(d) Does this not lead again to placing the Resolution of the League before the people of the zones concerned as a whole for acceptance?

As I write this letter and imagine the working of the Resolution in practice, I see nothing but ruin for the whole of India. Believe me, I approach you as a seeker. Though I represent nobody but myself, I aspire to represent all the inhabitants of India, for I realize in my own person their misery and degradation, which is their common lot, irrespective of class, caste or creed. I know that you have acquired a unique hold on the Muslim masses. I want you to use your influence for their total welfare, which must include the rest.

In this hastily written letter, I have only given an inkling of my difficulty.

Yours sincerely,
M K GANDHI

IX

LETTER TO M A JINNAH

September 15, 1944

Dear Qaid-e-Azam,

I have yours of the 14th instant, I received at 9.40 am

I woke up at 3 am today to finish my promised letter on the Lahore Resolution.

There is no mistake about the date, for I wrote in answer to your reminder of the 13th instant.

Independence does mean as envisaged in the ALCC Resolution of 1942. But it cannot be on the basis of a united India. If we come to a settlement, it would be or the basis of the settlement, assuming, of course, that it accrues general acceptance in the country. The process will be somewhat like this. We reach by joint effort independence for India as it stands. India becoming free will proceed to demarcation plebiscite and partition if the people concerned vote for partition, all this is implied in the Rajaji Formula.

As to the provisional interim government, I am afraid I cannot carry my answer any further than I have done. Though I have no scheme for the provisional government, if you have one in connection with the Lahore Resolution, which also, I presume, requires an interim government, we can discuss it.

The Formula was framed by Rajaji in good faith. I accepted it in equal good faith. The hope was that you would look at it with favour. We still think it to be the best in the circumstances. You and I have to put flesh on it, we can. I explained the process we have to go through. I hope, you have no objection to it. Perhaps, you want to know how I would form the provisional government if I was invited there to. If I was in that unenviable position, I would see all the claimants and endeavour to satisfy them. My co-operation will be available in that task.

I can give you full satisfaction about your inquiry, "What I would like to know would be, what will be the powers of such a provisional interim government, how will it be formed, to whom it will it be responsible." The provisional interim government will be responsible to the elected members of the present Assembly or a newly elected one. It will have all the powers less that of the Commander-in-Chief during the war and full powers thereafter. It will be the authority to give effect to the agreement that may be arrived at between the League and the Congress and ratified by the other parties.

Yours sincerely,
M K GANDHI

X

LETTER FROM M A JINNAH

September 17, 1944

Dear Mr Gandhi,

I have your letter of September 15 and I thank you for it. I note that you have for the moment shunted the Rajaji Formula and are applying your mind very seriously to the Resolution of the Muslim League. It is my duty to explain the Lahore Resolution to you today and persuade you to accept it. This, even though you are talking to me, as you have often made it clear, in your individual capacity. I have successfully converted non-Muslim Indians in no small number and also a large body of foreigners, and if I can convert you, exercising as you do tremendous influence, over Hindu India, it will be no small assistance to me, although we are not proceeding on the footing that you are in carrying on these talks in your representative character or capacity, and my difficulties remain until you are vested with a representative status and authority in order to negotiate and reach an agreement with you.

You have stated in September 11 that the Lahore Resolution is 'indefinite'. I, therefore, naturally asked you to please let me know in what way or respect the Lahore Resolution is indefinite, and now I have received your letter of September 15 under reply.

The third paragraph of your letter is not seeking clarification, but a disquisition and expression of your views on the point, whether the Mussalmans are a nation.

This matter can hardly be discussed by means of correspondence. There is a great deal of discussion and literature on this point which is available, and it is for you to judge finally, when you have studied this question thoroughly, whether the Mussalmans and Hindus are not two major nations in this sub-continent. For the moment, I would refer you to two publications, although there are many more Dr Ambedkar's book and MRT's *Nationalism in Conflict* in India. We maintain and hold that Muslims and Hindus are two major nations by any definition or test of a nation. We are a nation of hundred million, and what is more, we are a nation with our own distinctive culture and civilization, language and literature, art and architecture, names and nomenclature, sense of values and proportion, legal laws and moral codes, customs and calendar, history and traditions, aptitudes and ambitions. In short, we have our own distinctive outlook on life and of life. By all canons of international law we are a nation.

Now I shall reply to your various points:

1. Yes, the word 'Pakistan' is not mentioned in the Resolution and it does not bear the original meaning. The word has now become synonymous with the Lahore Resolution.
2. This point does not arise, but still I reply that the question is a mere bogey.
3. This point is covered by my answer that the Mussalmans of India are a nation. As to the last part of your query, it is hardly relevant to the matter of clarification of the Resolution.
4. Surely, you know what the word 'Muslims' means.
5. This point does not arise by way of clarification of the text of the Lahore Resolution.
6. No. They will form units of Pakistan.
7. As soon as the basis and the principles embodied in the Lahore Resolution are accepted, the question of demarcation will have to be taken up immediately.
8. In view of my reply to (7), your question (8) has been answered.
9. Does not relate to clarification.
10. My answer to (9) covers this point.
11. Does not arise out of the clarification of the Resolution. Surely, this is not asking for clarification of the Resolution. I have in numerous speeches of mine and the Muslim League in its resolutions have pointed out that this is the only solution to India's problem and the road to achieve freedom and independence of the peoples of India.
12. 'Muslims under the Princes': The Lahore

Resolution is only confined to British India. This question does not arise out of clarification of the Resolution.

13. The definition of 'minorities': You yourself have often said minorities mean "accepted minorities".
14. The adequate, effective and mandatory safeguards for minorities referred to in the Resolution are a matter for negotiation and settlement with the minorities in the respective States, viz., Pakistan and Hindustan.
15. It does give basic principles and when they are accepted, the details will have to be worked out by the contracting parties.

(a & b). Does not arise by way of clarification;

(c) The Muslim League is the only authoritative and representative organization of Muslim India;

(d) No. See answer (c).

As regards your final paragraph, before receiving clarifications from me, you have already passed your judgment and condemned the Lahore Resolution, when you say, 'As I write the letter and imagine the working of the Resolution in practice I see nothing but ruin for the whole of India.' I understand that you have made clear to me that you represent nobody but yourself, and I am trying to persuade you and to convert you that this is the road which will lead us all to the achievement of freedom and independence, not only of the two major nations, Hindus and Muslims, but of the rest of the peoples of India, but when you proceed to say that you aspire to represent all the inhabitants of India, I regret I cannot accept that statement of yours. It is quite clear that you represent nobody else but the Hindus, and as long as you do not realize your true position and the realities, it is very difficult for me to argue with you, and it becomes still more difficult to persuade you, and hope to convert you to the realities and the actual conditions prevailing in India today. I am pleading before you in the hope of converting you, as I have done with many others successfully.

As I have said before, you are a great man and you exercise enormous influence over the Hindus, particularly the masses, and by accepting the road that I am pointing out to you, you are not prejudicing or harming the interests of the Hindus or of the minorities. On the contrary, Hindus will be the greater gainers. I am convinced that true welfare not only of the Muslim but the rest of India lies in the division of India as proposed by the Lahore Resolution. It is for you to consider whether it is not your policy and programme, in which you have persisted, which has been the principle factor of ruin of the whole of India and of misery and degradation of the people to which you refer and which I deplore no less than anyone else. And it is for that very reason I am pleading before you all these days, although you insist that you are having talks with me only in your individual capacity, in the hope that you may yet revise your policy and programme.

Yours sincerely,
JINNAH

XI

LEITER TO M A JINNAH

September 19, 1944

Dear Qaid-e-Azam,

Many thanks for yours of the 17th instant.

I am sorry to have to say that your answers omitting 1, 2 and 6 do not give satisfaction.

It may be that all my questions do not arise from the view of mere clarification of the Lahore Resolution. But I contend that they are very relevant from the standpoint of a seeker that I am. You cannot expect anyone to agree to or shoulder the burden of the claim contained in the Lahore Resolution without, for instance, answering my questions 15 (a) and 15 (b) which you brush aside as not arising by way of clarification.

Dr Ambedkar's thesis, while it is ably written, has carried no conviction to me. The other book mentioned by you, I am sorry to say, I have not seen.

Why can you not accept my statement that I aspire to represent all the sections that compose the people of India? Do you not aspire? Should not every Indian? That the aspiration may never be realized is beside the point.

I am beholden to you, in spite of your opinion about me, for having patience with me. I hope you will never lose it, but will persevere in your effort to convert me. I ask you to take me with my strong views and even prejudices, if I am guilty of any. As to your verdict on my policy and programme, we must agree to differ. For, I am wholly unrepentant. My purpose is as a lover of communal unity to place my services at your disposal.

I hope you do not expect me to accept the Lahore Resolution without understanding its implications. If your letter is the final word, there is little hope. Can we not agree to differ on the question of "two nations" and yet solve the problem on the basis of self-determination? It is this basis that has brought me to you. If the regions holding Muslim majorities have to be separated according to the Lahore Resolution, the grave step of separation should be specifically placed before and approved by the people in that area.

Yours sincerely,
M K GANDHI

XII

LETTER FROM M A JINNAH

September 21, 1944

Dear Mr Gandhi,

I am in receipt of your letter of September 19, and I have already given you my answers to all your questions relating to clarification of the Lahore Resolution or any part of it, and I am glad that you admit when you say it may be that "all my questions do not arise from the view of mere clarification of the Lahore Resolution", but you particularly emphasize your points 15 (a) and 15 (b).

I regret to say, it has no relation to the context of the Resolution or any part thereof. You have brought so many matters into our correspondence, which are entirely outside the matter requiring clarification, so I have perforce to deal with them. Let me first deal with your letter of September ll.

1. You say, 'My life mission has been Hindu-Muslim unity, which I want for its own sake but which is not to be achieved without the foreign ruling power being ousted.' Hence the first condition of the exercise of the right of self-determination is achieving independence by the joint action of all the parties and groups composing India. If such joint action is unfortunately impossible, then too I must fight with the assistance of such elements as can be brought together.
2. The gist of your letters up to date is that you are wedded to this policy and will pursue it. In your next letter of September 14, while you were good enough to furnish me with the clarification of the Gandhi-Rajaji Formula, you were pleased to observe: 'I have, at any rate, for the moment put it out of my mind and I am, now concentrating on the Lahore Resolution in the hope of .finding a ground for mutual agreement.'

In your letter of September 15, you say, 'Independence does mean as envisaged in the AICC Resolution of 1942.' It is, therefore, clear that you are not prepared to revise your policy and that you adhere firmly to your policy and programme, which you have persisted in and which culminated in your demand, final policy, programme and the method and sanction for enforcing it by resorting to mass civil disobedience in terms of the August 8, 1942, Resolution, and you have made it clearer again by stating in your letter of September 19 as follows: 'As to your verdict on my policy and programme, we must agree to differ. For, I am wholly unrepentant.' You know that the August 1942 Resolution is inimical to the ideals and demands of Muslim India.

Then again, in the course of our discussion when I asked you for clarification of the Gandhi-Rajaji Formula, you were pleased to say, by your letter of September 15 as follows: 'For the moment I have shunted the Rajaji Formula and with your assistance am applying my mind very seriously to the famous Lahore Resolution of the: Muslim League.' We discussed it in its various aspects, as you told me you were open to be persuaded and converted to our point of view. I discussed the Resolution at great length with you, and explained everything you wanted to understand, even though you have emphasised more than once that you are having these talks with me in your personal capacity, and in your letter of September 15 you assured me in the following words with regard to the Lahore Resolution, 'Believe me, I approach you as a seeker, though I represent nobody but myself,' and that you were open to conviction and conversion.

You had informed me by your letter of September 11 as follows: 'It is true that I said an ocean separated you and me in outlook. But that had no reference to the Lahore Resolution of the League. The League Resolution is indefinite.' I naturally, therefore, proceeded in reply to ask you by my letter of September 11 as follows: 'You say the Lahore Resolution is indefinite. You never asked me for any clarification or explanation of the terms of the Resolution, but you really indicated your emphatic opposition to the very basis and the fundamental principles embodied in it. I would, therefore, like to know in what way or respect the Lahore Resolution is indefinite.' And I sent you a reminder on September 13, to which you replied by your letter of September 15, not confining yourself really to matters of clarification, but introducing other extraneous matters, with some of which I had already dealt, in reply to this letter of yours of September 15, by my letter of September 17 and furnished you with all the clarifications, informing you that you had introduced several matters which could hardly be discussed in a satisfactory manner by means of correspondence. I have already given you all the clarifications you require so far as the Lahore Resolution goes and its text is concerned.

You, again raise further arguments, reasons and grounds and continue to persist in a disquisition on the point, amongst others, whether Muslims of India are a nation, and then you proceed further to say; 'Can we not agree to differ on the question of two nations and yet solve the problem on the basis of self-determination?' It seems to me that you are labouring under some misconception of the real meaning of the word - 'self-determination'. Apart from the inconsistencies and contradictions of the various positions that you have adopted in the course of our correspondence, as indicated above, can you not appreciate our point of view that we claim the right of self-determination as a nation and not as a territorial unit, and that we are entitled to exercise our inherent right as a Muslim nation, which is our birthright?

Whereas you are labouring under the wrong idea that 'self-determination' means only that of 'a territorial unit' which, by the way, is neither demarcated nor defined yet and there is no Union or Federal Constitution of India in being, functioning as a sovereign Central

Government. Ours is a case of division and carving out of two independent sovereign States by way of settlement between two major nations, Hindus and Muslims, and not of severance or secession from any existing union, which is non-existent in India. The right of self-determination, which we claim, postulates that we are a nation, and as such it would be the self-determination of the Mussalmans, and they alone are entitled to exercise that right.

I hope you will now understand that your question 15(a) does not arise out of the Lahore Resolution or of any part thereof. As to 15(b), again it does not arise as a matter of clarification, for it will be a matter for the constitution-making body chosen by Pakistan to deal with and decide all matters as a sovereign body representing Pakistan vis-a-vis the constitution-making body of Hindustan or any other party concerned. There cannot be Defence and similar matters of 'common concern' when it is accepted that Pakistan and Hindustan will be two separate independent sovereign States. 1 hope, I have now given all satisfactory explanations, over and above the matter of clarification of the Lahore Resolution, in the hope of converting you as an individual 'seeker'.

Yours sincerely,
JINNAH

XIII

LETTER TO M A JINNAH

September 22, 1944

Dear Qaid-e-Azam,

Your letter of yesterday, 21st instant, so disturbed me that I thought I would postpone my reply till after we had met at the usual time. Though I made no advance at our meeting, I think I see somewhat clearly what you are driving at. The more I think about the two-nation theory the more alarming it appears to be. The book recommended by you gives me no help. It contains half truths and its conclusions or inferences are unwarranted. I am unable to accept the proposition that the Muslims of India are a nation, distinct from the rest of the inhabitants India. Mere assertion is no proof. The consequences of accepting such a proposition are dangerous in the extreme. Once the principle is admitted there would be no limit to claims for cutting up India into numerous divisions, which would spell India's ruin. I have, therefore, suggested a way out. Let it be a Partition as between two brothers, if a division there must be.

You seem to be averse to a plebiscite. In spite of the admitted importance of the League, there must be clear proof that the people affected desire Partition. In my opinion, all the people inhabiting the area ought to express their opinion specifically on this single issue of division. Adult suffrage is the best method, but I would accept any other equivalent.

You summarily reject the idea of common interest between the two arms. I can be no willing party to a division which does not provide for the simultaneous safeguarding of common interests, such as Defence, Foreign Affairs and the like. There will be no feeling of security by the people of India without recognition of the neutral and mutual obligations arising out of physical contiguity.

Your letter shows a wide divergence of opinion and outlook between us. Thus you adhere to the opinion often expressed by you that the August 1942 Resolution is 'inimical to the ideals and demands of Muslim India'. There is no proof for this sweeping statement.

We seem to be moving in a circle. I have made a suggestion. If we are bent on agreeing, as I hope we are, let us call in a third party or parties to guide or even arbitrate between us.

Yours sincerely,
M K GANDHI

XIV

LETTER FROM M A JINNAH
September 23, 1944

Dear Mr Gandhi,

I am in receipt of your letter of September 22 and thank you for it. I am sorry that you think 1 have summarily rejected the idea of common interest between two arms and now you put it somewhat differently from 15(a), when you say there will be no feeling of security by the people of India without recognition of the natural and mutual obligations arising out of physical contiguity. My answer, already given, is that it will be for the constitution-making body of Pakistan and that of Hindustan, or any other party concerned, to deal with such matters on the footing of their being two independent States.

I am really surprised when you say there is no proof of what you characterise as a sweeping statement of mine, that the August 1942 Resolution inimical to the ideals and demands of Muslim India. The Resolution in its essence is as follows:

(a) Immediate grant of Complete Independence [and] setting up immediately of a Federal Central Government on the basis of a united, democratic Government of India with federated units or Provinces, which means establishing a Hindu Raj.

(b) That this National Government so set up will evolve a scheme for a Constituent Assembly, which will be chosen by adult franchise, which will prepare a constitution for the Government of India, which means that the Constituent Assembly chosen will be composed of an overwhelming majority of the Hindus, nearly 75 percent.

(c) To enforce this demand of the Congress the August Resolution decides on and sanctions a resort to mass civil disobedience at your command and when ordered by you as the sole Dictator of the Congress.

This demand is basically and fundamentally opposed to the ideals and demands of Muslim India of Pakistan, as embodied in the Lahore Resolution and to enforce such a demand by means of resort to mass civil disobedience is inimical to the ideals and demands of Muslim India, and if you succeed in realizing this demand it would be a death-blow to Muslim India. I see from the correspondence and talks between you and me that you are still holding fast to this fateful resolution.

From the very first day of our talks, you made it dear to me, and you have repeatedly said in the course of our correspondence and talks that you have approached me in your individual capacity, and you assured me that you were a seeker of light and knowledge and that you seriously and earnestly wanted to understand the Lahore Resolution and were open to conviction and conversion.

Therefore, in deference to your wishes I made every effort all these days and in the course of our prolonged talks and correspondence to convert you, but unfortunately it seems I have failed. And now you have made new suggestions and proposals by your letter under reply.

1. You say, "I have, therefore, suggested a way out. Let it be a Partition as between two brothers, if a division there must be". I really do not know what this means and I would like you to elaborate this proposal and give me some rough outlines of this new idea of yours, as to how and when the division is to take place, and in what way it is different from the division envisaged by the Lahore Resolution.
2. You say, "Let us call a third party or parties to guide or even arbitrate between us". May I point out that you have repeatedly made clear to me that you are having these talks as an individual seeker? How can any question of a third party or parties to guide or arbitrate between us arise?

Yours sincerely,
JINNAH

XV

LETTER TO M A JINNAH

September 23, 1944

Dear Qaid-e-Azam,

Last evening's talk has left a bad taste in the mouth. Our talks and our correspondence seem to run in parallel lines and never touch one another. We reached the breaking point last evening but, thank God, we were unwilling to part. We resumed discussion and suspended it in order to allow me to keep time for the evening public prayer.

In order that all possibility of making any mistake in matter of this great importance may be removed I would like to give me in writing what precisely on your part you want me to put my signature to. I adhere to my suggestion that we may call in some outside assistance to help us at this stage.

Yours sincerely,

M K GANDHI

XVI

LETTER TO M A JINNAH

September 24, 1944

Dear Qaid-e-Azam,

I have your two letters of September in reply to my letters of the 22nd and 23rd.

With your assistance, I am exploring the possibilities of reaching an agreement, so that the claim embodied in the Muslim League Resolution of Lahore may be reasonably satisfied. You must, therefore, have no apprehensions that the August Resolution will stand in the way of our reaching an agreement. That Resolution dealt with the question of India as against Britain, and I cannot stand in the way of our settlement.

I proceed on the assumption that India is not to be regarded as two or more nations, but as one family consisting of many members of whom the Muslims living in the north-west zones, i.e, Baluchistan, Sind, North-West Frontier Province and that par of the Punjab where they are in absolute majority over all the other elements and in parts of Bengal and Assam where they are in absolute majority, desire to live in separation from the rest of India.

Differing from you on the general basis, I can yet recommend to the Congress and the country the acceptance of the claim for separation contained in the Muslim League Resolution of Lahore, 1940, on my basis and on the following terms:

The areas should be demarcated by a commission, approved by the Congress and the League. The wishes of the inhabitants of the area demarcated should be ascertained through the votes of the adult population of the areas or through some equivalent method.

If the vote is in favour of separation, it shall be agreed that these areas shall form a separate State as soon as possible after India is free from foreign domination and can, therefore, be constituted into two sovereign independent States.

There shall be a treaty of separation, which should also provide for the efficient and satisfactory administration of Foreign Affairs, Defence, Internal Communications, Customs, Commerce and the like, which must necessarily continue to be matters of common interest between the contracting parties.

The treaty shall also contain terms for safeguarding the rights of minorities in the two States.

Immediately on the acceptance of this agreement by the Congress and the League, the two shall decide upon a common course of action for the attainment of the independence of India.

The League will, however, be free to remain out of any direct action, to which the Congress may resort and in which the League may not be willing to participate.

If you do not agree to these terms, could you let me know in precise terms what you would have me to accept in terms of the Lahore Resolution and bind myself to recommend to the Congress? If you could kindly do this, I shall be able to see, apart from the difference in approach, what definite terms I can agree to.

In your letter of 23rd September, you refer to 'the basis and fundamental principles embodied in the Lahore Resolution' and ask me to accept them. Surely, this is unnecessary when, as I feel, I have accepted the concrete consequence that should follow from such acceptance.

Yours sincerely,
M K GANDHI

XVII

GANDHIJI TO RAJAJI

Talk with M A Jinnah

September 24, 1944

[JINNAH:] "If you want defence and so many things in common, that means that you visualise a centre?"

[GANDHI:] "No, but I must say, in practice, there will have to be a body selected by both parties to regulate these things."

Then he came to the August (1942) Resolution. He said it was inimical to Muslims.

"But don't you see that it is absolutely a baseless charge. With all the legal acumen that is attributed to you, why cannot you see that it deals with only India and the British rule? It has nothing to do with the Muslims. You can refer the matter to a lawyer of eminence impersonally and take his opinion whether there is anything in it which could be considered inimical to that Muslim League or the Muslims."

He said he did not need to do so. "Why should I want another's opinion when I know it for myself?" I broached the subject that I had fixed up to be at Sevagram on the 2nd October. I would like to leave on the 30th and would be back in four or five days. He said, "Why must we take so long? We had better close up now. I will have everything ready on Tuesday. You will examine the copies and I will do so." He had the introduction also ready and read it out. I said I had nothing to say against it, but if I had a copy I could examine it. He said could do so on Tuesday. I said all right. He would not have a third party, nor would he produce his own scheme. He condemned the August Resolution. He suggested in so many words that amends should be made, i.e., it should be retracted.

XVIII

LETTER FROM M A JINNAH

September 25, 1944

Dear Mr Gandhi,

I am in receipt of your letter of September 24, and I thank you for it. You have already rejected the basic and fundamental principles of the Lahore Resolution.

1. You do not accept that the Mussalmans of India are a nation.
2. You do not accept that the Mussalmans have an inherent right of self-determination.
3. You do not accept that they alone are entitled to exercise this right of theirs for self-determination.
4. You do not accept that Pakistan is composed of two zones, northwest and north-east, comprising six Provinces, namely, Sindh, Baluchistan, North-West Frontier Provinces, Punjab, Bengal and Assam, subject to territorial adjustments that may be agreed upon, as indicated in the

> Lahore Resolution. The matter of demarcating and defining the territories can be taken up after the fundamentals above mentioned are accepted, and for that purpose, machinery may be set up by agreement. You do not accept the provisions embodied in the Lahore Resolution for safeguarding the minorities.

I asked you ... to give me rough outlines of this new idea of yours as to how and when the division is to take place and in what way it is different from the division envisaged in the Lahore Resolution, and now you have been good enough to give me your amplification, in your letter of September 24 under reply....

The terms clearly indicate that your basis is in vital conflict with and is opposed to the fundamental basis and principles of the Lahore Resolution.

Now let me take your main terms:

(a) 'I proceed on the assumption that India is not to be regarded as two or more nations, but as one family consisting of many members, of whom the Muslims living in the north-west zones, i.e., Baluchistan, Sindh, North- West Frontier Province and that part of the Punjab where they are in absolute majority over all the other elements and in parts of Bengal and Assam where they are in absolute majority, desire to live in separation from the rest of India.' If this term were accepted and given effect to, the present boundaries of these Provinces would be maimed and mutilated beyond redemption and leave us only with the husk, and it is opposed to the Lahore Resolution.

(b) That, even in these mutilated areas so defined; the right of self determination will not be exercised by the Muslims but by the inhabitants of these areas so demarcated. This again is opposed to the fundamentals of the Lahore Resolution.

(c) That, if the vote is in favour of separation, they shall be followed to 'form a separate State as soon as possible after India is free from foreign domination', whereas we propose that we should come to a complete settlement of our own immediately and by our united front and efforts do everything in our power to secure the freedom and independence of the peoples of India on the basis of Pakistan and Hindustan.

(d) Next you say, 'There shall be a treaty of separation which should also provide for the efficient and satisfactory administration of Foreign Affairs, Defence, Internal Communications, Customs, Commerce, and the like, which must necessarily continue to be matters of common interest between the contracting parties.' If these vital matters are to be administered by some central authority, you do not indicate what sort of authority or machinery will be set up to administer these matters, and how and to whom again that authority will be responsible. According to the Lahore Resolution, as I have already explained to you, all these matters, which are the life-blood of any State, cannot be delegated to any central authority or government. The matter of security of the two States and the natural and mutual obligations that may arise out of physical contiguity will be for the constitution-making body of Pakistan and that of Hindustan, or [any] other party concerned, to deal with on the footing of their being two independent States. As regards the safeguarding of the rights of minorities, I have already explained that this question of safeguarding the minorities is fully stated in the Lahore Resolution.

You will, therefore, see that the entire basis of your new proposal is fundamentally opposed to the Lahore Resolution, and as I have already pointed out to you both in the correspondence and in our discussions, it is very difficult for me to entertain counter-proposals and negotiate ... unless they come from you in your representative capacity. That was the same difficulty with regard to the Gandhi-Rajaji Formula, and I made it clear to you, at the very outset, but the Formula was discussed as you asserted that it had met the Lahore Resolution in substance. But while you were furnishing me with the clarification of this Formula, you shunted it and we confined ourselves to the Lahore Resolution, and hence the question of your representative capacity did not arise regarding this Formula. But now you have, in your letter of September 24, made a new proposal of your own on your own basis, and the same difficulties present themselves to me as before, and it is difficult to deal with it any further unless it comes from you in your representative capacity.

I cannot agree with you when you finally wind up by saying: "In your letter of 23rd September, you refer to the basic and fundamental principles embodied in the Lahore Resolution' and ask me to accept them. Surely, this is unnecessary when as I feel I have accepted the concrete consequence that should follow from such acceptance." This is obviously far from correct. Why not then accept the fundamentals of the Lahore Resolution and proceed to settle the details?

Yours sincerely
JINNAH

XIX

LETTER TO M A JINNAH

September 25, 1944

Dear Qaid-e-Azam,

Yesterday's talk leads me to inflict this. I trust you will not mind.

Our conversations have come about as a result of your correspondence with Rajaji in July last, over his Formula and your consultations with the League Working Committee thereon, and my own letter to you suggesting a meeting between you and me. My proposal of yesterday is an earnest effort to meet the essential requirements of the Lahore Resolution. I would like you, therefore, to think fifty times before throwing away an offer which had been made entirely in the spirit of service in the cause of communal harmony. Do not take, I pray, the responsibility of rejecting the offer. Throw it on your Council. Give me an opportunity of addressing them. If they feel like rejecting it, I would like you to advise the Council to put it before the open session of the League. If you will accept my advice and permit me, I would attend the open session and address it.

You are too technical when you dismiss my proposal for arbitration or outside guidance over points of difference. If I have approached you as an individual, and not in any representative capacity, it is because we believe that if I reach an agreement with you, it will be of material use in the process of securing a Congress League settlement and acceptance of it by the country. Is it irrelevant or inadmissible to supplement our efforts to convince each other without help, guidance, advice or even arbitration?

Yours sincerely,
M K GANDHI

XX

LETTER FROM M A JINNAH
September 26, 1944

Dear Mr Gandhi,

I am in receipt of your letter of September 25. It is entirely incorrect and has no foundation in fact, for you to say that our conversations have come about as a result of my correspondence with Rajaji in July last over his Formula. It is equally baseless to say 'and your consultations with the League Working Committee thereon'. It was entirely in response to your letter of July 17, 1944, which I received while I was at Srinagar, with a fervent request on your part to meet you, and you ended that letter by saying, "Do not disappoint me." In my reply, again from Srinagar, dated July 24, 1944, I intimated to you that I would be glad to receive you at my house in Bombay on my return, which would probably be about the middle of August.

This was long before the meeting of the Working Committee or that of the Council of the All-India Muslim League, and long before I reached Lahore, and when you arrived here and told me that you were approaching me in your individual capacity, I at once made it clear to you and informed you, both in our talks and by my letter, that the position you had taken up had no precedent for it, and further that it was not possible to negotiate and reach an agreement unless both the parties were fully represented. For, it is one-sided business, as it will not be binding upon any organisation in any sense whatever, but you would as an individual only recommend it, if any agreement is reached, to the Congress and the country, whereas it would be binding upon me as the President of the Muslim League. I cannot accept this position. I hope you do see the unfairness and the great disadvantage to me, and it is so simple and elementary for anyone to understand.

As regards your proposal of yesterday, which you have simplified in your letter of September 24, I have already sent you my reply.

With regard to your suggestion to be allowed to address the meeting of the Council, and if they feel like rejecting your 'offer' the matter should be put before the open session, let me inform you that only a member or delegate is entitled to participate in the deliberations of the meetings of the Council or in the open session respectively. Besides, it is a most extraordinary and unprecedented suggestion to make. However, I thank you for your advice.

As regards your proposal for arbitration and outside guidance, I have already replied to you, and it is not merely technical but a matter of substance. I fully reciprocate your desire for securing a Congress-League settlement.

However, I regret I have failed to convince you and convert you, as I was hopeful of doing.

Yours sincerely,
JINNAH

XXI

LETTER TO MA JINNAH

September 26, 1944

Dear Quaid-e-Azam,

In view of my letter to you of yesterday, left to myself, I would have refrained from dealing with your letter before our meeting today. But I have deferred to Rajaji's advice to finish the chain of correspondence.

I confess I am unable to understand your persistent refusal to appreciate the fact that the Formula presented to you by me in my letter of the 24th as well as the Formula presented to you by Rajaji give you virtually what is embodied in the Lahore Resolution, providing at the same time what is absolutely necessary to make the arrangement acceptable to the country. You keep on saying that I should accept certain theses, while I have been contending that the best way for us, who differ in our approach to the problem, is to give body to the demand as it stands in the Resolution and work it out to our mutual satisfaction. It is on this plan that I understand Rajaji's Formula is to be conceived, and it is on the same plan that I have tried to work it out in the course of and as a result of our talks. I contend that either gives you the substance of the Lahore Resolution. Unfortunately, you reject both. And I cannot accept the Lahore Resolution as you want me to especially when you seek to introduce into its interpretation theories and claims which I cannot accept and which I cannot ever hope to induce India to accept.

Your constant references to my not being clothed with representative authority are really irrelevant. I have approached you so that, if you and I can agree upon a common course of action, I may use what influence I possess for its acceptance by the Congress and the country. If you break, it cannot be because I have no representative capacity, or because I have been unwilling to give you satisfaction in regard to the claim embodied in the Lahore Resolution.

Yours sincerely,
M K GANDHI

XVII

LETTER FROM M A JINNAH
September 26, 1944

Dear Mr Gandhi,
I have received your letter of September 26, and I note that you have written it with Rajaji's advice. Of course, it is for you to follow such advice as you may choose to do, but I am only concerned for the moment with you.

I note that at the last moment you have resurrected the Gandhi-Rajaji Formula, although it was shunted all this time and you proceed to say that this Formula gives me virtually what is embodied in the Lahore Resolution. You further say that on the same plan you have tried to formulate your latest proposals, as mentioned your letter of September 24 and you maintain that either gives me the substance of the Lahore Resolution.

In your previous letter you asserted that your Formula gives me the "essence" of the Lahore Resolution.

I see a very close family resemblance between the two, and the substance of one or the other is practically the same, only it is put in different language, and I have already expressed my opinion, that in my judgment they neither meet the substance nor the essence of the Lahore Resolution. On the contrary, both are calculated to completely torpedo the Pakistan demand of Muslim India. I have never asked you to accept certain theses nor have I introduced any theories in the Lahore Resolution. Theses and theories are matters for scholars to indulge in.

I am very sorry I have to repeat, but I am compelled to do so, that I cannot agree with you that my references to your not being clothed with representative authority are really irrelevant. On the contrary, they have an important bearing, as I have already explained to you more than once. You again repeat that if you and I can agree upon a common course of action, you may use what influence you possess for its acceptance by the Congress and the country. I have already stated from the very beginning that that is not enough, for the reasons I have already given. Your representative capacity comes into play when you are making counter-proposals, and I cannot understand how you can say that it is irrelevant. No responsible organisation can entertain any proposal from any individual, however great he may be, unless it is backed up with the authority of a recognized organisation, and comes from its fully accredited representative. However, I need not labour this point any more, as I have already explained it in our previous correspondence.

If a break comes, it will be because you have not satisfied me in regard to the essence of the claim embodied in the Lahore Resolution. It is not a question of your being unwilling, but in fact, it is so. If a break comes it will be most unfortunate. If one does not agree with you or differs from you, you are always right and the other party is always wrong, and the next thing is that many are waiting prepared, in your circle, to pillory me when the word goes, but I must face all threats and consequences, and I can only act according to my judgment and conscience.

Yours sincerely,
JINNAH

XVIII

M A JINNAH'S STATEMENT

September 27, 1944

Mr Gandhi from the very commencement of our talks made it clear that he had approached me in his individual capacity and that he represented no one but himself. However, he assured me that he was really open to conviction and conversion to the Muslim League Lahore Resolution of March, 1940.

Without prejudice to my objection that in order to reach any settlement, negotiations can only be carried on properly when the other side is also fully represented and vested with authority, in deference to Mr Gandhi's wishes, I agreed to the task of persuading and converting him to the fundamentals of the Lahore Resolution.

I have placed before him everything and every aspect of the Muslim point of view in the course of our prolonged talks and correspondence, and we discussed all the pros and cons generally and I regret to say that I have failed in my task of converting Mr Gandhi.

We have, therefore, decided to release to the Press the correspondence that has passed between us.

Nevertheless, we hope that the public will not feel embittered, and we trust that this is not the final end of our effort.